A RUMOR
of ANGELS

QUOTATIONS FOR LIVING, DYING & LETTING GO

Revised edition

GAIL PERRY JOHNSTON
& JILL PERRY RABIDEAU

Cupola
PRESS™

www.cupolapress.com

© 2007 by Gail Perry Johnston

Published in Lafayette, California by Cupola Press™

The first edition of this book was published in 1989 by Random House, Inc.

Permission Acknowledgments appear on page 163.

Library of Congress Control Number: 2007900567

ISBN-13: 978-0-9793345-0-4
ISBN-10: 0-9793345-0-0

Printed in the United States of America

This book is dedicated to the big hearts
of Uncle Richard, Aunt Rosemary and Pops.

C O N T E N T S

Preface: 3

CHAPTER ONE: PAGE 5

Living

CHAPTER TWO: PAGE 59

Dying

CHAPTER THREE: PAGE 99

Letting go

Acknowledgements: 163

PREFACE

We all die, but few of us care to think about it. So, at first glance, an inspirational book on such a grievous subject may seem incongruous. But *A Rumor of Angels* isn't entirely about death. It's about the way we choose to live in the face of death, whether our own or that of a loved one. Within these pages the words of literary masters and contemporary figures have been gathered to form an easily accessible source of courage, insight, and comfort.

The book is divided into three chapters.

CHAPTER ONE focuses on the gift of life and the ways in which life becomes more precious as we acknowledge our finitude and the finitude of those close to us. Selected passages challenge us to discover what is ultimately important during a time when superficiality has no place.

CHAPTER TWO addresses grief and its many underlying dark emotions, such as guilt, anger, and depression. These passages explore the need to accept and share our human responses, for to ignore them only irritates and perpetuates inner pain.

CHAPTER THREE brings us into the light again. Selections speak encouragingly to those whose death is imminent, as well as to those who must carry on after severe loss. They offer not a series of pat answers and clichés, but sincere experiences and moving convictions.

Please note that *A Rumor of Angels* does not glamorize death, or pretend that it's anything other than cruel. Maybe the reason why death is so ugly and uncomfortable is because men and women, as originally designed by God, were not created to die. Death does not suit us, no matter who we are or what our age is. We were created to live, and even though death has long since entered our world, we know inside that something just isn't right about it, and certainly, it should not be the last word on our existence.

Anyone willing to work through a great loss; anyone striving to make sense out of it; and anyone wanting to believe in the rumor of angels, will find encouragement and truth in the voices that follow.

Living

Living

"You're an angel," blurted Jan's husband.

"An angel!" I thought angrily. How could I be an angel? I put Jan through three months of rigorous rehabilitation. Yet, within just ten days from her discharge home, she collapsed. Now, after six more grueling months of hospitalization, I felt like a failure. Almost shamefully I protested, "I wish I could have done so much more! I am *no* angel."

I teach my patients "quality" living, that it's the life in our years that counts; not the years in our life. I speak of the intangibles—love, inner beauty, memories—that outlast time. Do I believe it all?

Jan's husband rewinds my spirit: "You gave my wife back to me for ten days. They were such wonderful days at home. And for this I can never thank you enough."

CHAPTER ONE is about living and loving, though your own days, or the days of your loved one, may be as few as ten.

Living . . . To appreciate special moments and to maintain your spirit and character may not seem possible or even desirable when you are amid desperation. But Chapter One, in its entirety, will fill you with encouragement and confidence to live fully even now.

Loving . . . To share/bear each other's burdens and to communicate honestly and openly with each other may be a challenge beyond your strength. But Chapter One will guide the love in you to meaningful expressions and actions. The poetry and prose will assure you of the worth and foreverness of love. As inner beauty can transcend a damaged body, so can love transcend death.

*D*uration is not a test of true or false. The day of the dragon-fly or the night of the Saturnid moth is not invalid simply because that phase in its life cycle is brief. Validity need have no relation to time, to duration, to continuity.

ANNE MORROW LINDBERGH, *Gift From The Sea*

*T*he advantage of living is not measured by length, but by use; some men have lived long, and lived little; attend to it while you are in it.

MICHEL EYQUEM DE MONTAIGNE

*W*hen you work in the hospital a lot, you do sometimes find yourself imagining how you would act in those extreme situations [of your own death].... I end up hoping that I would have ... courage manifested not in wise, comforting speeches or saintly joy in the inevitable, but in the maintenance of spirit and individuality in impossible circumstances. Not to mention humor, of whatever kind.

PERRI KLASS, *A Not Entirely Benign Procedure*

*H*ope means to keep living
amid desperation
and to keep humming
in the darkness.

HENRI J.M. NOUWEN, *With Open Hands*

*O*n the day of his death, when his mother came into his room in the morning, the young boy spoke his last words. She asked him what he wanted for breakfast, and his reply was, "A kiss."

SANDOL STODDARD, referring to a 14-year-old hospice guest

*A*nd yet." Those are my two favorite words, applicable to every situation, be it happy or bleak. The sun is rising? And yet it will set. A night of anguish? And yet it, too, will pass. The important thing is to shun resignation, to refuse to wallow in sterile fatalism.

ELIE WIESEL, *All Rivers Run to the Sea: Memoirs*

On Herb's last Thursday, I stopped by his hospital room, really just to ask how he was, and the intensive-care nurse encouraged me to go in.

Herb nodded when I said hello. Then I made some foolish, awkward, hospital visitor talk and conversation and Herb tried to smile and mouth an answer, but the muscles of his face couldn't quite make it. His breath wasn't there either.

Instead, he managed to move his hands somehow, and put them in front of him and pantomimed his familiar typing motion. Then he stopped and gave me a thumbs up.

The incredible Herb Caen was trying somehow to tell me to be of good cheer—to tell me the column would go on.

BILL GERMAN

It is better to light one candle than to curse the darkness.

ELEANOR ROOSEVELT

We who lived in concentration camps can remember the men who walked through the huts comforting others, giving away their last piece of bread. They may have been few in number, but they offer sufficient proof that everything can be taken from a man but one thing: the last of human freedoms—to choose one's attitude in any given set of circumstances, to choose one's own way.

VICTOR FRANKEL

*A*nd there is a Catskill eagle
in some souls that can alike dive down
into the blackest gorges, and soar out
of them again and become invisible
in the sunny spaces.

HERMAN MELVILLE, *Moby-Dick*

I encourage such patients to set
goals that are three months, six
months, and a year into the future.
Sometimes they protest that they'll
never live that long, but my reply is
that none of us know how long we
will live. In the face of that uncertainty,
it is still healthy to have things to look
forward to, and commitments to the
future can be powerfully energizing....

STEPHANIE MATTHEWS SIMONTON,
The Healing Family

*N*ow is not the time to think of what you do not have.
Think of what you can do with what there is.

ERNEST HEMINGWAY, *The Old Man and the Sea*

*D*on't let the uncertainty turn you around
Go on and make a joyful sound
Into a dancer you have grown
From a seed somebody else has thrown
Go on ahead and throw some seeds of your own
And somewhere between the time you arrive
And the time you go
May lie a reason you were alive

JACKSON BROWNE, from the song, "For A Dancer"

*W*hen one door of happiness closes, another opens; but often
we look so long at the closed door that we do not see the one
which has been opened for us.

HELEN KELLER

*T*hus says Yahweh,
who made a way through the sea,
a path in the great waters....
"See, I am doing a new deed,
even now it comes to light; can you not see it?
Yes, I am making a road in the wilderness,
paths in the wilds."

ISAIAH 43:16, 19, *The Jerusalem Bible*

*D*ying is a wild night and a new road.

EMILY DICKINSON

I was ever a fighter, so—one fight more,
    The best and the last!
I would hate that death bandaged my eyes, and forebore,
    And bade me creep past....
For sudden the worst turns the best to the brave,
    The black minute's at end,
And the elements' rage, the fiend-voices that rave,
    Shall dwindle, shall blend,
Shall change, shall become first a peace out of pain,
    Then a light, then thy breast,
O thou soul of my soul! I shall clasp thee again,
    And with God be the rest.

ROBERT BROWNING, from "Prospice"

*Y*ou asked me about my families. Women up here speak of their first family, their second family, their third family. Counting the baby boy I lost that first winter, I've had four families. Nine children. They're out there." I knew what she meant, the little graveyard we'd passed on the way in....

"Katherine Mary, we're going to know each other very well, for many years, I hope. You'll come to understand. These big things, these terrible things, are not the important ones. If they were, how could one go on living? No it is the small, little things that make up a day, that bring fullness and happiness to a life. Your Sergeant coming home, a good dinner, your little Mary laughing, the smell of the woods—oh, so many things, you know them yourself." She took my hand.

BENEDICT and NANCY FREEDMAN, *Mrs. Mike*

_To_ see a world in a grain of sand
And a heaven in a wild flower,
Hold infinity in the palm of your hand
And eternity in an hour

WILLIAM BLAKE

_We_ often fantasize about a perfect day—something
exotic and far away. But when it comes to those we miss,
we desperately want one more familiar meal, even one more
argument. What does this teach us? That the ordinary is
precious. That the normal day is a treasure.

MITCH ALBOM

What is life? It is the flash of a firefly in he night. It is the
breath of a buffalo in the winter time. It is the little shadow
which runs across the grass and loses itself in the sunset.

CROWFOOT, Canadian Indian, dying words

There is not enough darkness in all the world to put out
the light of one small candle…. In moments of discouragement,
defeat or even despair, there are always certain things to cling
to. Little things usually: remembered laughter, the face of a
sleeping child, a tree in the wind—in fact, any reminder of
something deeply felt or dearly loved. No man is so poor as
not to have many of these small candles. When they are
lighted, darkness goes away and a touch of wonder remains.

ARTHUR GORDON, _A Touch of Wonder_

The light shines in the darkness,
and the darkness has not overcome it.

JOHN 1:5

Candlelight, in the Jewish faith,
symbolizes the human being. The wick
is the body. The flame is the soul that
strives upward.

ANONYMOUS

$\mathcal{I}$want to tell you about the good things
    I have experienced,
    not just the disappointments I've encountered.
The happy words I've shared,
    not the hostile outbursts.
The gentle touches I've given a friend,
    not the insensitive back I turned.
The pride I've rightly felt,
    not the boastful one-upmanship.
I need to be reminded of my personal worth,
    not to review my failures.
So help me God.

SANDRA ANN MCCORMICK BROOKS

$\mathcal{I}$used to think that life was hills and valleys—you go
through a dark time, then you go to the mountaintop, back
and forth. I don't believe that anymore.

Rather than life being hills and valleys, I believe that it's
kind of like two rails on a railroad track, and at all times
you have something good and something bad in your life.
No matter how good things are in your life, there is always
something bad that needs to be worked on. And no matter
how bad things are in your life, there is always something
good you can thank God for.

RICK WARREN

*M*y brother's death has taught me .... how important each of us is to everyone with whom we have contact, particularly our families and friends. The grief that overwhelmed my family indicated how much meaning Joe had added to our lives....
I rejoice that my brother Joe strove so earnestly to be caring and to develop his great talents. But I grieve that he did not seem to value the appreciation of those around him. If he had, perhaps he would not have taken himself from us.

I have learned through Joe's death to value the contribution I make to the lives of others, and the contribution they make to my life. We have not made ourselves; we are the gift of the living God to one another.

REINE DUELL BETHANY, referring to the suicide of her brother who had been a prominent member of the New York City Ballet

*N*o man is an island, entire of itself; every man is a piece of the continent, a part of the main; if a clod be washed away by the sea, Europe is the less, as well as if a promontory were, as well as if manor of thy friends or of thine own were; any man's death diminished me, because I am involved in mankind; and therefore never send to know for whom the bell tolls; it tolls for thee.

JOHN DONNE

To appreciate beauty; to find the best in others; to give one's self; to leave the world a little better; whether by a healthy child, a garden patch, or a redeemed social condition; to have played and laughed with enthusiasm, and sung with exultation; to know even one life has breathed easier because you have lived ... This is to have succeeded.

RALPH WALDO EMERSON

If I can stop one Heart from breaking
I shall not live in vain
If I can ease one Life the Aching
Or cool one Pain
Or help one fainting Robin
Unto his Nest again
I shall not live in Vain

EMILY DICKINSON

Lord, Make me an instrument of Thy peace.
Where there is hate, may I bring love;
Where offense, may I bring pardon;
May I bring union in place of discord;
Truth, replacing error;
Faith, where once there was doubt;
Hope, for despair;
Light, where was darkness;
Joy to replace sadness.
Make me not to so crave to be loved as to love.
Help me to learn that in giving I may receive;
In forgetting self, I may find life eternal.

ST. FRANCIS OF ASSISI

"You have been my friend,"
replied Charlotte. "That in itself is a
tremendous thing. I wove my webs
for you because I liked you. After all,
what's a life anyway? We're born, we
live a little while, we die. A spider's
life can't help being something of
a mess, with all this trapping and
eating flies. By helping you, perhaps
I was trying to lift up my life a trifle.
Heaven knows anyone's life can
stand a little of that."

E.B. WHITE, *Charlotte's Web*

Two days later, in the evening, I entered her bedroom. She was resting fairly comfortably. As was my custom, I looked at the growing mountain of cards she received. There was one in a red envelope, unopened. It was addressed to me. I opened it. It said, "Happy Birthday." By her own hand (that was obviously shaking) she had written, "I'll always love you," and, as if she could write no more, an almost illegible signature, "Beth." Even in her anguish she had thought of me. She had had a nurse get the card and then managed to write her last written words by herself.

WILLARD K. KOHN, *The Widower*

Death is a challenge. It tell us not to waste time.... It tells us to tell each other right now that we love each other.

LEO F. BUSCAGLIA, *Living, Loving & Learning*

My daughter has Cystic Fibrosis, a life-threatening disease. But I don't really think about losing her. What I think about is the possibility of losing any one of my three children on any given day, due to a car accident, fall or something unknown. But I'm not a *worried* mother. I'm a *grateful* mother—grateful for the gift of each day we have together.

LYNN BLOMQUIST

But death does not stand at the end of life, it is all through it. It is the fear of losing, the knowledge of losing that makes love tender.

BENEDICT and NANCY FREEDMAN, *Mrs. Mike*

I was thinking this evening I have always felt that I would give almost anything to have another five minutes with my father to say good-bye. Not so with Lucas. He got everything I had to give from the day of his birth until the hour of his death. There was nothing left unsaid. I treasured every moment with him and felt his unqualified love in return. Only this knowledge allows me to heal.

GORDON LIVINGSTON, after losing his 6 year old son

We call her Mrs. Fixer because she fixes
   Everything for everybody.
If you need a ride, you call her,
   Or a meal, or a telephone committee.
She'll find you an apartment or a part-time job,
   Even a date if you're in the market.
And all the time she only wants someone to love her
   But she's afraid to ask.
So she fixes everything for everybody instead
And you keep calling her when you need something
   And forget to tell her that you love her.
So she'll probably die lonely
   And have a big funeral
And everyone will tell about
   The way she fixed things all the time.

JAMES KAVANAUGH, "Mrs. Fixer", *Will You Be My Friend?*

If this day should come to an end and we don't tell you at least once that we love you, you'll be disappointed, the world will be less and we will be less.

BRENNAN MANNING

*H*ere death makes its greatest gift, for the sure and ever-present awareness that I shall die much sooner than I would wish, and that others are moving as quickly and surely to the same end, enhances all human relationships from that of casual acquaintance to that of deepest love.... If only we can learn to act as if we are going to die then death loses much of its power over us.... If we realize that love is stronger than death, we may see that length of life is not important.

BETTY R. GREEN and DONALD P. IRISH

and now you and i am now and we're
a mystery which will never happen again,
a miracle which has never happened before—
and shining this our now must come to then

E.E. CUMMINGS

He was harsh and visibly angry with us—not because he was dying, but because he felt that we were not "living." He told us that we looked at him and thought "this poor young man is dying," while we ignored the fact that we too were dying. He told us that he was the only one around who was truly alive, aware of the preciousness of each moment.

LISL MARBURG GOODMAN, PH.D., *Death and the Creative Life*

He who would teach men to die would teach them to live.

MICHEL EYQUEM DE MONTAIGNE

In my happier days I used to remark on the aptitude of the saying, "When in life we are in the midst of death." I have since learnt that it's more apt to say, "When in death we are in the midst of life."

A BELSEN SURVIVOR

If one truly grasped all of this, what would the consequences be?... The radical uncertainty of death ... makes the moment precious and therefore beautiful. It can free us from procrastination, the illusion that we have an infinite amount of time, that we can put off living until some future time—after graduation, or after career and financial security are obtained, or after a particular project is finished, or after a special relationship is established.... Earnest thought about one's own death does not make one fearfully or morbidly preoccupied with death, for earnestness makes one realize that time is too precious to be spent being morbid. It does not lead to a giving up of plans or projects, though it does change the mental frame of reference within which they are chosen and worked on. It does not mean one lives every day *simply* as if it were one's last—a kind of crazy living "for the moment" rather than living "in the moment".... To live "in the moment" means to be gracefully present to the simplest and most complex joys and tasks. It means to value the "dailiness of life."

MARCUS BORG

Sitting in a graveyard you involuntarily cast your mind back over all your past life, your past actions, and your plans for the future. And here you do not lie to yourself as you do so often in life, because you feel as if all those people sleeping the sleep of peace around you were somehow still present, and you were conversing with them. Sitting in a graveyard you momentarily rise above your daily ambitions, cares and emotions—you rise for an instant even above yourself.

ALEXANDER SOLZHENITSYN

Frequently in my Pursuits of whatever Kind,
let this come into my Mind;
"How much shall I value this on my Death Bed?"

JONATHAN EDWARDS, from his diary

As a physician who has been deeply privileged to share the most profound moments of people's lives, including their final moments, let me tell you a secret. People facing death don't think about what degrees they have earned, what positions they have held or how much wealth they have accumulated. At the end, what really matters—and is a good measure of a past life—is who you loved and who loved you.

BERNADINE HEALY, M.D.

re you getting well?"

"No," Emma said. "I have a million cancers. I can't get well."

"Oh, I don't know what to do," Teddy said …

"Well, both of you better make some friends," Emma said. "I'm sorry about this, but I can't help it. I can't talk to you too much longer either, or I'll get too upset. Fortunately we had ten or twelve years and we did a lot of talking, and that's more than a lot of people get.… "

When they came to hug her, Teddy fell apart and Tommy remained stiff.

"Tommy, be sweet," Emma said. "Be sweet, please. Don't keep pretending you dislike me. That's silly."

"I like you," Tommy said, shrugging tightly.

"I know that, but for the last year or two you've been pretending you hate me," Emma said. "I know I love you more than anybody in the world except your brother and sister, and I'm not going to be around long enough to change my mind about you. But you're going to live a long time, and in a year or two when I'm not around to irritate you you're going to remember that I read you a lot of stories and made you a lot of milkshakes and allowed you to goof off a lot when I could have been forcing you to mow the lawn."

Both boys looked away, shocked that their mother's voice was so weak.

"In other words, you're going to remember that you love me," Emma said. "I imagine you'll wish you could tell me that you've changed your mind, but you won't be able to, so I'm telling you now I already know you love me, just so you won't be in doubt about that later. Okay?"

"Okay," Tommy said quickly, a little gratefully.

LARRY McMURTRY, *Terms of Endearment*

if there are any heavens my mother will (all by herself) have one.

E.E. CUMMINGS

TO MY DEAR AND LOVING HUSBAND

If ever two were one, then surely we.
If ever man were lov'd by wife, then thee.
If ever wife was happy in a man,
Compare with me ye women if you can.
I prize thy love more than whole mines of gold,
Or all the riches that the East doth hold.
My love is such that Rivers cannot quench,
Nor ought but love from thee, give recompense.
Thy love is such I can no way repay,
The heavens reward thee manifold, I pray.
Then while we live, in love let's so persevere,
That when we live no more, we may live ever.

ANNE BRADSTREET

Many waters cannot quench love,
Nor will rivers overflow it....

SONG OF SOLOMON 8:7

Love is the only thing that we can carry with us when we go.

LOUISA MAY ALCOTT, *Little Women*

He went before she did.
She thought she would break.
She felt she was fallin' apart.
But still she remembers
The last words he said
As he held her hand close to his heart,

"I'm gonna hold on to you
Till the moon flies away
till the sky isn't blue,
I'm gonna hold on to you
Till the angels come call
Till the truth isn't true,
I'm gonna hold on to you."

WILLY WELCH

It should be my wishing,
That I might die with kissing.

BEN JOHNSON

But try love is a durable fire,
    In the mind ever burning.
Never sick, never old, never dead,
    From itself never turning.

SIR WALTER RALEIGH

*L*ove is patient, love is kind.... It always protects, always trusts, always hopes, always perseveres. Love never fails.... And now these three remain: faith, hope and love. But the greatest of these is love.

I CORINTHIANS 13:4, 7, 13, *NIV*

I remember those long, early morning walks we took together. We were both filled with a new awareness. We gloried in the smell of grass newly mown. We laughed to think that we had never really listened to the birds singing. Nothing and no one was ugly to us because this was life, and whatever came later, we had realized that what we had together was special and it could never be taken from us.

As the cancer grew within me, my body became misshapen and ugly, but it didn't make any difference to you. You said, "I love what you are and that makes you always beautiful to me." Then I realized how foolish I was and fell asleep with a smile on my face because your love did not waver.

BETH, cancer patient quoted by ELISABETH KÜBLER-ROSS

*A*nd I have found that the longer we have been married, and the more deeply I love him, the less I "see" him visually. "Close your eyes," I'm in the habit of telling my students of all ages, "and think about the person you love most in the world. Do you really see him visually? Or don't you see on a much deeper level?"

MADELEINE L'ENGLE, *A Circle of Quiet*

$\mathcal{W}$hat is REAL?" asked the Rabbit one day.

"Real isn't how you are made," said the Skin Horse. "It's a thing that happens to you. When a child loves you for a long, long time, not just to play with, but REALLY loves you, then you become Real."

"Does it hurt?" asked the Rabbit.

"Sometimes," said the Skin Horse, for he was always truthful. "When you are Real you don't mind being hurt."

"Does it happen all at once, like being wound up," he asked, "or bit by bit?"

"It doesn't happen all at once," said the Skin Horse. "You become. It takes a long time … Generally, by the time you are Real, most of your hair has been loved off, and your eyes drop out and you get loose in the joints and very shabby. But those things don't matter at all, because once you are Real you can't be ugly, except to people who don't understand."

MARGERY WILLIAMS, *The Velveteen Rabbit*

$\mathcal{I}$ think God has planned the strength and beauty of youth to be physical. But the strength and beauty of age is spiritual. We gradually lose the strength and beauty that is temporary so we'll be sure to concentrate on the strength and beauty which is forever.

J. ROBERTSON McQUILKIN

$\mathcal{G}$oodbye," said the fox. "And now here is my secret, a very simple secret: It is only with the heart that one can see rightly; what is essential is invisible to the eye."

ANTOINE DE SAINT-EXUPÉRY, *The Little Prince*

I gazed at her intently and saw that those eyes, which a few days ago were smiling like lips and moving like the wings of a nightingale, were already sunken and glazed with sorrow and pain. Her face, that had resembled the unfolding, sunkissed leaves of a lily, had faded and become colorless…. Her neck, that had been a column of ivory, was bent forward as if it no longer could support the burden of grief in her head.

All these changes I saw in Selma's face, but to me they were like a passing cloud that covered the face of the moon and makes it more beautiful.

KAHLIL GIBRAN, *The Broken Wings*

How beautifully the leaves grow old.
How full of light and colour are their last days.

JOHN BURROUGHS

Beauty here is not a matter of tidy appearances, logical properties, or even of physical prowess. Rather, it pertains to those exchanges between people, living and dying, who value one another as vessels of a purer and a more lasting force….

SANDOL STOPPARD, *The Hospice Movement*

My trial was to keep seeing her, to find her amid the grotesque distortions of disease…. It was the hardest thing I've ever done.

LE ANNE SCHREIBER

The jagged, ugly cancer sore went no deeper than my flesh.
There was no cancer in my Spirit.

THOMAS A. DOOLEY, *Doctor Tom Dooley, My Story*

Therefore we do not lose heart. Though outwardly we
are wasting away, yet inwardly we are being renewed day
by day....For what is seen is temporary, but what is unseen
is eternal.

II CORINTHIANS 4:16, 18, *NIV*

Prostrate, self-scorning,
Wingless and mourning,
Dust in the dust,
We lie as we must;
Empty. To dare not,
Know not and care not
Is our employ.
God, do Thou dower us,
Kindle, empower us,
Give us Thy joy.
Impotence clings—
How shall we bear it?
Wings, give us wings,
Wings of the spirit!

DMITRY MEREZHKOVSKY, "Prayer For Wings"

I am 78—and at my age I find that I have now taken in more than 1,000 tons of water, food, and air, the chemistry of which is temporarily employed for different lengths of time as hair, skin, flesh, bone, blood, etc., then progressively discarded. I weighed in at 7 pounds, and I went on to 70, then 170, and even 207 pounds. Then I lost 70 pounds, and I said, "Who was the 70 pounds?—because here I am...."

I am certain that I am not the avoirdupois of the most recent meals I have eaten, some of which will become my hair, only to be cut off twice a month. This lost 70 pounds of organic chemistry obviously wasn't "me," nor are any of the remaining presently associated atoms "me." We have been making a great error in identifying "me" and "you" as these truly transient and, ergo, sensorially detectable chemistries.... The only difference manifest between weight before and after death is that caused by air exhaled from the lungs....

Whatever life is, it doesn't weigh anything.

Buckminster Fuller

*M*ethinks my body is but the less of my better being.

Herman Melville, *Moby Dick*

*F*or so long my self-image depended on my physical strength and fitness. Now I'm being forced to far deeper dimensions.

Tim Hansel, *You Gotta Keep Dancin'*

For seven days we watched her life slowly ebbing. Only once did she make an effort to speak. The nurse and I were standing on either side of her bed watching, when she opened her glazing eyes and gasped, "so–a–ashamed–shamed."

The nurse, knowing what she meant, stooped down and kissed her saying with tears in her voice, "You don't need to be ashamed of anything. We nurses are all glad to do whatever we can for you."

HUGH TAYLOR

Blessed are those who heal us of self-despisings. Of all services which can be done to man, I know of none more precious.

WILLIAM HALE WHITE

Know deep down that you're worth any trouble you cause."

"You never told me that before." Peg's face cracks, into tiny pieces of stained glass, each piece glistening with moisture....

MEG WOODSON, referring to her 12-year-old daughter who has cystic fibrosis

A trauma can do one of two things: It can drive your family apart if you close communication and build walls, or it can pull your family closer together if you open communication lines and build bridges of love between one another.

PAM W. VREDVELT, Empty Arms

Compassion means to lay a bridge over to the other without knowing whether he wants to be reached.

HENRI J. M. NOUWEN, *With Open Hands*

But for me, fear is today and dying is now. You slip in and out of my room, give me medications and check my blood pressure. Is it because I am a student nurse, myself, or just a human being, that I sense your fright? And your fear enhances mine. Why are you afraid? I am the one who is dying!

I know, you feel insecure, don't know what to say, don't know what to do. But please believe me, if you care, you can't go wrong. Just admit that you care.

ANONYMOUS

If someone is dying and those around them insist that they do not die, the person dies in isolation, alone and without the love that can offer such support and such a sense of completion…. Truly, you can't go through the door with her, but you can accompany her more fully to the threshold.

STEPHEN LEVINE, *Meetings At The Edge*

Hope means that at the end I will not be rejected.

ELISABETH KÜBLER-ROSS

$\mathcal{I}$t is hoped that … our next generation of children will never again have to see a sign, "No Children Under Age 14 Allowed in the Hospital." It is hoped that all the children of our next generation will be permitted to face the realities of life. It is hoped that we will not "protect" them as a reflection of our own fears and our own anxieties!

ELISABETH KÜBLER-ROSS, *To Live Until You Say Goodbye*

$\mathcal{R}$emember: the child has experienced the worst possible tragedy. She should feel terrible. If she is sent off to summer camp to forget and deny, she will not learn that she can, in fact, tolerate and overcome emotional catastrophes. Permitting the child to feel the loss when she is ready will increase her coping ability for the rest of her life.

DR. ROBERTA TEMES, *Living With An Empty Chair*

$\mathcal{L}$et us not forget that in the nineteenth century, death … had become an occasion for the most perfect union between the one leaving and those remaining behind. The last communion with God and/or with others was the great privilege of the dying. For centuries there was no question of depriving them of this privilege.

PHILIPPE ARIES, *The Hour of Death*

*E*ven if death need not be welcomed, it need not always be opposed. But to stop the battle does not mean to abandon the patient or to cease caring for the patient. Caring continues even when the patient is allowed to die.

James Childress

*W*e should be more concerned with care, not cure.

Daniel Callahan

*L*iving and dying isn't easy. I'd like to see fewer courses and lectures (including my own) and see more painful waits beside the bed, more agonizing silences in the waiting....

John Langone

*T*he nearest friends can go
With anyone to death, comes so far short
They might as well not try to go at all.
No, from the time when one is sick to death,
One is alone, and he dies alone.
Friends make pretence of following to the grave,
But before one is in it, their minds are turned
And making the best of their way back to life
And living people, and things they understand.

Robert Frost

*E*ven these may forget, but I will not forget you.
"Behold, I have inscribed you on the palms of My hands."

Isaiah 49:15-16, *New American Standard Bible*

And know that I am with you always; yes, to the end of time.

MATTHEW 28:20, *The Jerusalem Bible*

As I once died, you too must pass away.
But trust my singing promise as your own.
My melody shall sound above the fray
Of battlefields: you shall not die alone.

CALVIN MILLER, *The Finale*

There was silence for a long time. I held her hand. It was hard and soft and brittle. After a while she looked at me again.

"I guess I'm going to leave," she said.

"I know," I said.

"I'm very tired."

"I know," I said again.

"I never died before," she smiled again a little bit.

"I've never been with someone who died before," I said.

"I think we'll make it, Pastor." She was almost whispering. She squeezed my hand a little.

"Will you listen while I pray?" Her eyes closed. I did not answer. She knew what I would say.

"My Father," she whispered, "take me home because of my Jesus, and Father, take care of this good boy here. He has given love, and he has been my friend. Amen."

TED SCHROEDER

A friend loves at all times, and a brother is born for adversity.

PROVERBS 17:17, *NIV*

Communion between men (in infantry battalions) is as profound as any between lovers. Actually, it is more so.... It is, unlike marriage, a bond that cannot be broken by a word, by boredom or divorce, or by anything other than death. Sometimes even that is not strong enough. Two friends of mine died trying to save the corpses of their men from the battlefield. Such devotion, simple and selfless, the sentiment of belonging to each other, was the one decent thing we found in a conflict otherwise notable for its monstrosities.

PHILIP CAPUTO, *A Rumor of War*

Shared suffering, shared fear make a stronger bond than blood. Pain cracks us wide open and is totally revealing, and this is when we learn what we really love and this is what we never forget.

AGNES DE MILLE, *Reprieve*

Love is what you've been through with somebody.

JAMES THURBER

They say that the tree of loving
Grows on the Bank of the River of Suffering.

PETER YARROW, from the song, "Weave me the Sunshine"

She and I are two unhappy ones who keep together and carry our burdens together, and in this way unhappiness is changed to joy, and the unbearable becomes bearable.

VINCENT VAN GOGH

The talk broke over Penny in a torrent. The relief of words washed and cleansed a hurt that had been in-growing. He listened gravely, nodding his head from time to time. He was a small staunch rock against which their grief might bear. When they finished and fell quiet, he talked of his own losses. It was a reminder that no man was spared. What all had borne, each could bear. He shared their sorrow, and they became a part of his, and the sharing spread their grief a little, by thinning it.

MARJORIE KINNAN RAWLINGS, *The Yearling*

Rejoice with those who rejoice; mourn with those who mourn.

ROMANS 12:15, *NIV*

My mother was very happy as I sat by her. But I think she knew death was near, for she said strange things to me—things touching the emotions that she would never have dared say otherwise, for affection between parents and children was never shown among my people. She called me "my daughter"— a thing she had never said before in her life.

AGNES SMEDLEY, *Daughter of Earth*

Man's feelings are always purest and most glowing in the hour of meeting and of farewell.

JEAN PAUL RICHTER

O, but they say the tongues of dying men
Enforce attention like deep harmony.
Where words are scarce they are seldom spent in vain,
For they breathe truth that breathe their words in pain.

WILLIAM SHAKESPEARE, *Richard II*

*O*ur last night together was spent by the pool. We talked late into the night. Just about little things but we really connected. It was as if she knew it would be our last opportunity to hang out together. It was her gift to me before she left.

BUSHRA ECKSTEIN

*T*he book on death, dying, life, after-life is in progress. We're taking home a paperback about the death of a cat. Perhaps it is lighter reading for the evening. No doubt it is insightful, for pets are often one's introduction to the story of separation.

A young woman and man pass us. Their walk is assured and high-spirited, as if to oppose the oncoming night and stillness of town activity. Three cats of grand character trail them. They follow at a respectable distance of one to two cat-lengths from each other. Their long-haired beauty is such that it would seem an offense not to acknowledge their presence. So, we stop for a while and watch, like tourists, the happy parade.

We no sooner turn to go on our way than a sudden screech and a heavy thump strike us like a whip to the back. The hindmost cat has been hit! Hit and run over with no warning, no mercy! Head to the street, its legs claw the air. Its nose and mouth give blood, eyes grow wider and wilder. The other cats close in. Only inches away, they watch the disjointed dance of death.

The young woman covers her mouth, screams a defiant No! Her eyes strain forward, but her legs are limp. The man races to the car. Yelling through the window, he insists the driver take their pet to the doctor—hospital—clinic—or somewhere *else*. He then straightens, businesslike, but remains distant. Why is he, why is she so far away? Far away from each other and far away from their cat, no longer clawing but breathing like a pump up and down. What do they fear? The ugliness of death—as if the misshapen body means their cat is suddenly a stranger? The guilt of death—as if the accident means they failed to be all-caring and protecting? Or the pronouncement of death—as if words would release a primordial curse on all of life?

They stand separated. Only the cats are near to each other, seeming to react honestly. If they had hands and arms, they would probably pick up and stroke the dying cat in its last moments of life. What they do, instinctively, it to be close, very close, and help their friend not to die alone.

Gail Perry Johnston and Jill Perry Rabideau

The dying need the community, its help and fellowship.... The community needs the dying to make it think of eternal issues and to make it listen.... We are debtors to those who can make us learn such things as to be gentle and to approach others with true attention and respect.

Dr. Cicely Saunders, founder of St. Christopher's Hospice in London

In the beginning of life, when we are infants, we need others to survive, right? And at the end of life, when you get like me, you need others to survive, right?"

His voice dropped to a whisper. "But here's the secret: in between, we need others as well."

MITCH ALBOM, *Tuesdays With Morrie*

But there is one thing we all can do, and that is to listen…. Most of us are passive listeners. Usually we're already thinking about our response, preparing our rebuttal. Our own thoughts and needs get in the way, and we don't even hear what is being said. When you are talking with someone who is approaching death or who lives day-to-day with the threat of death, you must listen with both ears wide open. And that isn't easy.

I find that if I sit directly across from someone and hold hands, then purge my mind of anything personal, I can hear some amazing things. When I'm listening aggressively I never intrude or comment on what is being said. I prod a little to keep the flow going, or I respond with a nod or a facial expression that indicates that I understand or that I don't. I reassure the speaker by patting his hand or holding it more tightly.

TED MENTEN

Most of us know how to say nothing, but few of us know when.

WES IZZARD, journalist and newscaster

$\mathcal{I}$t is no secret that many of our suggestions, advice, admonitions, and good words are often offered in order to keep distances rather than to allow closeness.... An old lady once told the following story:

I was so happy when one day a nice young student came to visit me and we had such a marvelous time. I told her about my husband and my children and how lonely and sad I often feel. And when I was talking, tears came out of my eyes, but inside I felt glad that someone was listening. But then—a few days later the student came back to me and said: "I have thought a lot about what you told me and about how you feel ... and I wonder if you might be interested in joining this club that we are having...." When I heard her saying this I felt a little ashamed, since I had caused so many worries for this good person, whereas the only thing I wanted was someone to listen and to understand.

HENRI J.M. NOUWEN and WALTER J. GAFFNEY, *Aging*

$\mathcal{L}$isten a hundred times; ponder a thousand times; speak once.

TURKISH PROVERB

$\mathcal{F}$inding solutions to problems is actually less important than affirming your love and concern. The greatest gift that you can give to a troubled individual is your presence. For it is the kind word that diminishes the pain, rekindles the hope, and finally generates a feeling of strength.

ROBERT L. VENINGA, *A Gift of Hope*

We found that when you are holding a hand, any hand, the parts of your brain responsible for mobilizing your body into action calm down.... The brain works a lot less hard when there is someone else helping us cope.

JAMES A. COAN, neuroscientist

Jerry Cook spoke to the congregation, saying: "Many of you know that John and Pam were expecting a baby. That baby is now with the Lord.... Now listen to me and listen well.... They don't need any 'words from God' or 'inspired exhortations,' or advice. They just need you to love them and hug them and let them work through their grief. There will be a point where sympathy will no longer be needed or wanted, so please be sensitive to them and just allow them to be themselves."

PAM W. VREDVELT

To handle yourself, use your head;
to handle others, use your heart."

ELEANOR ROOSEVELT

My own experience in grieving leads me to believe that written words can often be more comforting than face to face conversations. I can think of several occasions when friends or relatives with every good intention said the wrong thing, worsening the pain. Carefully expressed thoughts or quotes by insightful authors can be written out and then considered by the griever at a time when he or she is ready to receive them.

MARTIE SMITH

$\mathcal{T}$he older children felt the loss more deeply and for a longer period of time.... one day about a year after Beth died I had been to the cemetery and I came back feeling rather sad and lonely. I asked the girls if they ever went to the gravesite. They all answered that they did not. I am afraid I reacted very badly, making statements that never should have been said. Finally, the oldest girl, through tear-strained eyes, snapped at me, "You grieve any way you want, but we do not have to look at a grave to remember how much we miss and love Mother." They were right, and I have never questioned their method of expressing their grief again.

WILLARD K. KOHN, *The Widower*

$\mathcal{A}$my was a young artist who lived next door to me in East Lansing, Michigan. After her mother died in November, she lived alone with her father. On Mother's Day, six months after her mother's death, I saw Amy out in the yard cutting flowers. I walked over and said, "Hi, I just thought I'd come over and talk for a while. I know that it's your first Mother's Day without your mother, and you're probably feeling unhappy."

Tears came into Amy's eyes as she blurted out an immediate response to my words. "You're the first person all day who has even mentioned Mother's Day." she exclaimed. "Doesn't anyone know that it's Mother's Day and that I miss her?"... Her tears were appreciative tears. Someone was finally paying attention to the sad feelings and memories already stirring inside."

ANN KAISER STEARNS, *Living Through Personal Crisis*

*H*ad you restrained your love, you would be free of sorrow. The greater the love, while one possesses it, the greater the sorrow when one is deprived of it.

VON TEPL

*I*f it isn't just a meaningless form of words, I suppose my heart broke that night. It really means, though, loving past all measure.... For it had been death in love, not death of love. Love can die in many ways, most of them far more terrible than physical death ...

SHELDON VANAUKEN, *A Severe Mercy*

*T*he great tragedy of life is not that men perish, but that they cease to love.

W. SOMERSET MAUGHAM

One has to embrace the world like a lover. One has to accept pain as a condition of existence. One has to court doubt and darkness as the cost of knowing. One needs a will stubborn in conflict, but apt always to total acceptance of every consequence of living and dying.

MORRIS L. WEST, *The Shoes of the Fisherman*

Tell me how much you know of the sufferings of your fellow men and I will tell you how much you have loved them.

HELMUT THIELICKE, *Our Heavenly Father*

My Uncle Burke was a wealthy man. On his deathbed he said to me, "Sandra, money is the easiest thing you'll come by in life, but what really matters is the success of your relationships—relationships that take time and cause pain but are worth it nonetheless."

SANDRA SHEEHAN FISCHMAN

I hold it true, whate'er befall;
   I feel it, when I sorrow most;
   'Tis better to have loved and lost
Then never to have loved at all.

ALFRED, LORD TENNYSON

Let me come in where you sit weeping,
Let me, who have not any child to die,
Weep with you for the little one whose love
   I have known nothing of.

The little arms that slowly, slowly loosed
Their pressure round your neck; the hands you used
To kiss.—Such arms—such hands I never knew.
   May I not weep with you?

Fain would I be of service—say something,
Between the tears, that would be comforting,—
But ah! so sadder than yourselves am I,
   Who have no child to die.

JAMES WHITCOMB RILEY, "Bereaved"

*P*ains of love be sweeter far
Than all other pleasures are.

JOHN DRYDEN

*F*orget-me-nots—
Those beautiful, delicate, misty blue flowers
that drift like clouds
over our gardens in the Spring
Declaring love, remembrance—
and as every gardener knows
who has ever tried to get rid of them—
Constancy!

ELAINE BERGER

SHE DWELT AMONG THE UNTRODDEN WAYS

She dwelt among the untrodden ways
 Beside the springs of Dove,
A maid whom there were none to praise
 And very few to love,

A violet by a mossy stone
 Half hidden from the eye!
Fair as a star, when only one
 Is shining in the sky.

She lived unknown, and few could know
 When Lucy ceased to be;
But she is in her grave, and, oh,
 The difference to me!

WILLIAM WORDSWORTH

Stopped, his turning
Growth in time,
Forever now eighteen,
Forever muscled,
Mustached, moving
In our remembering minds.
Forever budding, burgeoning
His art, his thought, his life,
Never to unfold in flower
Or reach the summertime of fruit

LOLLY QUINONES

He wasn't my flesh and blood," said the Captain, looking at the fire—"I ain't got none—but somewhat of what a father feels when he loses a son, I feel in losing Wal'r. For why?" said the Captain. "Because it ain't one loss but a round dozen. Where's that there young school boy with the rosy face and curly hair, that used to be as merry in this here parlour, come round every week, as a piece of music. Gone down with Wal'r. Where's that there fresh lad, that nothing couldn't tire nor put out, and that sparkled up and blushed so when we joked him about Heart's Delight, that he was beautiful to look at? Gone down with Wal'r. Where's that there man's spirit, all afire, that wouldn't see the old man hove down for a moment, and cared nothing for itself? Gone down with Wal'r. It ain't one Wal'r. There were a dozen Wal'r that I knowed and loved, all holding round his neck when he went down, and they're a-holding round mine now.

CHARLES DICKENS, *Domby and Son*

Memories are little stabs around the heart.
It's hard to lose a friend!

JAMES KAVANAUGH, *Will You Be My Friend*

Six years have already passed since my friend went away from me.... If I try to describe him here, it is to make sure that I shall not forget him. To forget a friend is sad. Not everyone has had a friend.

ANTOINE DE SAINT-EXUPÉRY, *The Little Prince*

The heart that has truly loved never forgets.

THOMAS MORE

I'll remember you
And I'm sorry that the time we have is almost through
But the special thing that means so much
Is knowing we can really touch

RANDY STONEHILL

Everybody needs his memories.
They keep the wolf of insignificance from the door.

SAUL BELLOW

The "loved object is not gone," psychoanalyst Karl Abraham
writes, "for now I carry it within myself…." And while surely
he overstates—the touch is gone, the laugh is gone, the
promise and possibilities are gone, the sharing of music and
bread and bed is gone, the comforting joy-giving flesh-and-
blood presence is gone—it is true nonetheless that by making
the dead a part of our inner world, we will in some important
way never lose them.

JUDITH VIORST, *Necessary Losses*

No love, no friendship can cross the path of our destiny
without leaving some mark on it forever.

FRANCOIS MAURIAC

I don't ask for your pity, but your understanding—no, not even that—no. Just for your recognition of me in you....

Tennessee Williams

*N*o really great song can ever attain full purport till long after the death of its singer—till it has accrued and incorporated the many passions, many joys and sorrows, it has itself aroused.

Walt Whitman

*T*here were many such stories, and he understood how important they were, and listened with patience and with respect. A life without stories would be no life at all. And stories bound us, did they not, one to another, the living to the dead.

Alexander McCall Smith, *In The Company of Cheerful Ladies*

I don't believe you dead. How can you be dead if I still feel you? Maybe, like God, you changed into something different that I'll have to speak to in a different way, but you not dead to me Nettie. And never will be. Sometime when I git tired of talking to myself I talk to you.

Alice Walker, *The Color Purple*

*T*his is the last sentence Morrie got out before I did: "Death ends a life, not a relationship."

Mich Albom, *Tuesdays with Morrie*

In the dark immensity of night
I stood upon a hill and watched the light
Of a star,
Soundless and beautiful and far.

A scientist standing there with me
Said, "It is not the star you see,
But a glow
That left the star light years ago."

Men are like stars in a timeless sky:
The light of a good man's life shines high,
Golden and splendid
Long after his brief earth years are ended.

GRACE V. WATKINS

$\mathcal{B}$ut I don't understand. He is in heaven. He would be too happy to care for anything that is going on in this woeful world."

"Perhaps that is so," she said, smiling a sweet contradiction to her words, "but I don't believe it."

"What do you believe?"

"Many things that I have to say to you, but you cannot understand them now."

"I have sometimes wondered, for I cannot help it," I said, "whether he is shut off from all knowledge of me for all these years till I can go to him. It will be a great while. It seems hard. Roy would want to know something, if it were only a little, about me."

"I believe that he wants to know, and that he knows, Mary; though, since the belief must rest on analogy and conjecture, you need not accept it as demonstrated mathematics," she answered, with another smile.

"Roy never forgot me here!" I said, not meaning to sob.

"That's just it. He was not constituted so that he, remaining himself, Roy, could forget you. If he goes out into his other life forgetting, he becomes another than himself.... It seems to me to lie just here: Roy loved you. Our Father, for some tender, hidden reason, took him out of your sight for a while. Though changed much, he can have forgotten nothing. Being only out of sight, you remember, not lost, nor asleep, nor annihilated, he goes on loving. To love must mean to think of, to care for, to hope for, to pray for, not less out of body than in it."

ELIZABETH STUART PHELPS, *The Gates Ajar*

God forbid that on entering a happier life, I should become less loving, unfaithful to the memories and real joys of my other life.

Saint Augustine

They told me, Heraclitus, they told me
    you were dead.
They brought me bitter news to hear
    and bitter tears to shed.
I wept as I remembered how often
    you and I
Had tired the sun with talking
    and sent him down the sky.
And now that thou art lying, my dear
    old Carian guest,
A handful of gray ashes,
    long, long ago at rest,
Still are thy pleasant voices,
    the nightingale awake:
For Death, he taketh all away,
    but these he cannot take.

Callimachus, a Greek sculptor, about Heraclitus, a Greek philosopher, 3rd century B.C.

Daddy, I miss Mommy.

So do I, my child… so do I.

Daddy, when will Mommy come home?

She has gone to a new home in heaven, my child.

But Daddy, I want her to be here.

She is here, my child…in your heart. Can you feel her there?

Yes Daddy, but I want to touch her, I want her to hold me…

So do I, my child, so do I.

Daddy, I want to see Mommy.

Someday, my child, you will…

But Daddy, when?

Not for a long time, I pray…

But Daddy, someday, when I see her,

Will she remember me

Will she know who I am

Will she still love me?

Yes, my child…

she loves you now, and she will always love you…

and someday, when you see her again, the angels will sing

and you will feel love like you have never known before…

I want that now Dad.

So do I, my child, but you must be patient. For now you must feel the love that your mom left deep in your heart. That love will always be with you.

But it's hard for me Dad. Is it hard for you?

Yes it is, my child…yes it is.

GAROLD EDWARDS

*W*e give back, to you, Oh God, those whom you gave to us. You did not lose them when you gave them to us, and we do not lose them by their return to you.... Open our eyes to see more clearly, and draw us closer to you that we may know that we are nearer to our loved ones, who are with you.

WILLIAM PENN

*W*here we love is home,
Home that our feet may leave,
but not our hearts

OLIVER WENDELL HOLMES

CHAPTER TWO

Dying

The "weeping" willow tree is an ancient symbol of the house of mourning.

Dying

_R_ick refused to die. As cancer invaded his body, he experienced more pain than he had ever known in Vietnam. Yet, he pushed himself to move, talk, live. His goal was to get home to his wife and fourteen-month-old "miracle baby"—the baby he was told he never could have.

For three months I helped Rick fight. As my care for him grew, so did my torment. I wanted to tell him he would live, and feed his hope. I wanted to tell him he would not live and help him die.

Suddenly Rick's own thoughts were more than he could bear. Unable to share his fear and depression, he became hostile to everyone around him. For two weeks he refused to see his family.

Another medical emergency brought death closer than ever to Rick. An entire day passed before I found the courage to enter his room. He was quite alert, yet still. When I sat down beside him, he said, "Jill, please lay your head on my shoulder. Just for a minute. Please." I did....He cried.

We began a slow, painstaking conversation.

"How long are you going to live, Rick?"

"I don't know, Jill. I just don't know."

"Rick, what do you live for?"

"My wife. My baby. You know I live for my family."

"Then be with them, Rick."

"I hear you, Jill."

Within five minutes after I left, Rick's family arrived. Within one hour after I left, Rick died.

CHAPTER TWO is about fighting. We have been fighting death all our lives. At birth we fought death as we gasped for air in order to live. And now, if we accept Chapter One's encouragement to celebrate the gift of life, how can we not battle against the taker of life? Chapter Two does not romanticize death. Instead, selections boldly confront the tragedy in all its ugliness.

Rick's struggle involved turning away those closest to him. Suffering induces many moods and behaviors, sometimes ones that are entirely foreign to us. Certain quotes in Chapter Two may help you understand your own actions. Other quotes may help you understand those around you. You will not be informed of a right way to grieve. A struggle is a struggle. Chapter Two seeks only to relate to and demystify your experiences. Where there is clarity, there is comfort. Where there is understanding, there is withstanding.

Eventually Rick released his fears upon the shoulders of his loved ones. From Shakespeare to Anne Lamott we are told to "give sorrow words." Poetry and prose that encourage verbal expression, often coupled with tears, abound throughout history. Furthermore, much contemporary literature stresses the need to "work though" or "deal with" a grievous situation. One intent of Chapter Two is to explain just what that means. Though some comments may seem difficult to accept, do not be disheartened. Simply by reading *A Rumor of Angels,* you are boldly dealing with your own struggle.

The human mind is as little capable to contemplate death for any length of time as the eye is able to look at the sun.

LA ROCHEFOUCAULD

As men are not able to fight against death, misery, ignorance, they have taken it into their heads, in order to be happy, not to think about it at all.

BLAISE PASCAL

Go, go, go, said the bird; human kind
Cannot bear very much reality

T. S. ELIOT, from the poem, "Burnt Norton"

When we come across someone in great need, we often feel powerless. We hate to feel powerless so we look away.

PASTOR DEAN HONNETTE

Just realize, I am 69 and I have never seen a person die. I have never even been in the same house while a person died. How about birth? An obstetrician invited me to see my first birth only last year. Just think, these are the greatest events of life and they have been taken out of our experience. We somehow hope to live full emotional lives when we have carefully expunged the sources of the deepest human emotions.

GEORGE WALD, Nobel Prize Winner

Who is the happy, successful American? Answer this question by looking at the advertising in popular magazines. Notice the emphasis on youthfulness, vitality, and productivity. The worth of a man is measured by what he can produce. Doing is the criterion for being. Little wonder that Americans have such difficulty handling leisure time or retirement! I have a friend who spends every vacation in a remote wilderness spot, chopping wood and pumping water, and every year he returns from his vacation exhausted but released from the guilt he felt about taking time off work. Vitality is the foundation of this lifestyle. We place a huge premium on the aggressive, vigorous individual filled with boundless energy. Little wonder that death, the direct opposite of vital life, is denied.

RICHARD W. DOSS, *The Last Enemy*

So I'll continue to continue to pretend
My life will never end,
And flowers never bend
With the rainfall.

PAUL SIMON, from the song, "Flowers Never Bend With The Rainfall"

Death is a quiet person and kind of scary. He does not say much but is very sharp and it is almost impossible to outsmart him. Although you would like to stay away from him, there's something about him that kind of draws you to him. You like him and fear him at the same time. I picture Death as being millions of years old but only looking about forty.

ANONYMOUS

I know that I shall die soon and my mind is reconciled to it; but when I think that my body will be put into a coffin, that the lid of the coffin will be screwed down and I will be buried under the earth, I am horrified. I am well aware that my horror is unreasonable, that I shall not be feeling anything by then, but I cannot overcome this feeling. Sometimes I also have the feeling—and that is also unreasonable—that I shall not die. I read somewhere that a Frenchman had begun his will with the words: "Not when but if I should die one day...."

ALEXANDER SERVEYEVICH BUTURLIN, *Tolstoy Remembered By His Son*

*D*ying," he said to me, "is a very dull dreary affair." Suddenly he smiled. "And my advice to you is to have nothing whatever to do with it," he added.

SOMERSET MAUGHAM

*Y*et even our ties to earth-death are being systematically cut off. We neither kill nor harvest the food for our own tables. it comes to us already death-processed. We have no bone-deep knowledge that other things die so that we may eat and live.... Outside, the world itself dies every year. We have almost forgotten that. The sun withdraws its light, the darkness overshadows the earth. The waters freeze and the leaves decay. We forget because we don't have to live in that world anymore. We have created our own world where we have as much light and heat as we desire, hot running water, and fresh fruit the year round. We exempt ourselves from the season of death that envelops the world outside our artificial environment.

VIRGINIA STEM OWENS

_Tarry awhile, O Death, I cannot die
With all my blossoming hopes unharvested,
My joys ungarnered, all my songs unsung,
And all my tears unshed.
Tarry awhile, till I am satisfied
Of love and grief,
Of earth and altering sky;
Till all my human hungers are fulfilled,
O Death, I cannot die!

SAROJINI NAIDU

_When I realized that I was going to die, my first reaction
was not so much terror but affront. That this could happen
to me now, before I was ready, before I'd done the big works
I intended to do and was surely worthy of; that this could
happen unexpectedly and immediately to me, who had to be
present, of necessity, in order to notice, in order to keep track,
because, obviously, if I were not present I could not keep track,
and who, then, would? I had never thought consciously of
myself as important, but of course, in common with all other
humans, I felt that I was the pivot, the point of view, of the
world. And to think of life continuing in its daily way without
me there… was very nearly incomprehensible.

AGNES DE MILLE, *Reprieve*

_And does it not seem hard to you,
When all the sky is clear and blue,
And I should like so much to play,
To have to go to bed by day?

ROBERT LOUIS STEVENSON, *A Child's Garden of Verses*

*E*merging hopes and wishes
  Die like waves
  Leaving shore
And only moments before
  They were
Frothing and glistening.

WILLIAM J. RICE

*D*eath lies on her life an untimely frost
Upon the sweetest flower of all the field.

WILLIAM SHAKESPEARE, *Romeo and Juliet*

*D*eath is always and under all circumstances a tragedy, for if it is not, then it means that life itself has become one.

THEODORE ROOSEVELT

*D*idn't they realize that to die is to die, whether you are seventeen, forty-nine, or one hundred and ten? Didn't they know that our death is our death? And that each one of us has only one death to die? This was my father's death! It was no less significant because he was most of a hundred. It was his death. The only one he would ever have.

JOSEPH W. MATHEWS

*M*y God! My God!… I'm dying…. It may happen this moment. There was light and now there is darkness. I was here and now I'm going there!… There will be nothing…. Can this be dying? No, I don't want to!

LEO TOLSTOY, *The Death of Ivan Ilych*

*A*nd He withdrew from them about a stone's throw, and He knelt down and began to pray, saying, "Father, if Thou art willing, remove this cup from Me; yet not My will, but Thine be done." Now an angel from heaven appeared to Him, strengthening Him. And being in agony He was praying very fervently, and His sweat became like drops of blood, falling down upon the ground.

LUKE 22:41-44, *New American Standard Bible*

He who pretends to look on death without fear lies.
All men are afraid of dying, this is the great law of sentient
beings, without which the entire human species would soon
be destroyed.

JEAN-JACQUES ROUSSEAU

The adventurous life is not one exempt from fear, but
on the contrary, one that is lived in full knowledge of fears of
all kinds, one in which we go forward in spite of our fears.
Many people have the utopian idea that others are less afraid
than they are and they feel therefore that they are inferior.
All men are afraid, even desperately afraid…. Fear is a part
of human nature.

PAUL TOURNIER, *The Adventure of Living*

I'm not afraid to die. I just don't want to be there
when it happens.

WOODY ALLEN

The basis of optimism is sheer terror.

OSCAR WILDE

Whether or not we admit it to ourselves, we are all haunted
by a truly awful sense of impermanence. I have always had a
particularly keen sense of this at New York cocktail parties,
and perhaps that is why I drink the martinis almost as fast as
I can snatch them from the tray.

TENNESSEE WILLIAMS

I found out that no one is ever prepared for death
and that grief has nothing to do with intelligence.

DR. ROBERTA TEMES, *Living With An Empty Chair*

The attempt to ban death from our consciousness is not
only unsuccessful, but also detrimental to the quality of our
lives. Even if we succeed in repressing the content of our fears,
the feelings attached to it will manifest themselves in the form
of vague, free-floating anxiety. We can never get rid of the fear
unless we know what it is that we are fearing.

LISL MARBURG GOODMAN, PH.D., *Death and the Creative Life*

We ignore the outer darkness;
or if we cannot ignore it,
if it presses too insistently upon us,
we disapprove of being afraid.

ALDOUS HUXLEY

Many fears are born of fatigue and loneliness.
Beyond a wholesome discipline, be gentle with yourself.

MAX EHRMANN

We are so conditioned to "think positively" that many people
secretly believe that if they directly experience their fear and
acknowledge it to someone, they will collapse into it and never
get back out. Of course this is not true.

STEPHANIE MATTHEWS SIMONTON, *The Healing Family*

*W*hat a silly world we live in, where we believe that everything has to be on a high, joyous level all the time…. We learn that from the media. We turn on our television set and we see people giddy over cornflakes….

LEO F. BUSCAGLIA

*P*eople who get sick don't necessarily behave well…. People who are sick get pugnacious, or uncooperative, or desperately cranky. They yell at their relatives, complain about their nurses, accuse their doctors of incompetence. And somehow, through it all, I think many of us who take care of sick people preserve this idea that they have some responsibility to behave in an exemplary style…. I remember a four-year-old boy who was dying; he screamed and carried on and attacked any doctor who came near him. So we asked a child psychiatrist to come by and see him, and the child psychiatrist reported back to us that he was terrified of dying. "Actually, that's quite appropriate under the circumstances," the psychiatrist told us, gently.

PERRI KLASS, *A Not Entirely Benign Procedure*

*D*on't bother me, can't you see I am busy dying?

H.G. WELLS, last words

My heart is broken
It is worn out at the knees
Hearing muffled
Seeing blind
Soon it will hit the Deep Freeze
And something is cracking
I don't know where
Ice on the Sidewalk
Brittle branches
In the air.

SUZANNE VEGA, from the song, "Cracking"

$\mathcal{B}$ut all my energies, then and later, were exerted in holding myself together. I always had this Humpty Dumpty fantasy that if I allowed myself to crack, no one, not "all the King's men" could ever put me back together again. I'm beginning to learn how wrong I was. Emotions can strengthen you, not splinter you. To express emotions is healthier than to repress them.

LYNN CAINE, *Widow*

$\mathcal{W}$hile grief is fresh,
every attempt to divert it
only irritates.

SAMUEL JOHNSON

$\mathcal{T}$here's no pain so cutting
No battle as in vain
As the constant battle
To avoid the pain

JUSTIN McROBERTS, from the song, "Waiting on Your Love"

$\mathcal{B}$ecause our griefstricken emotions often cloud and distort reality, it is hard to acknowledge that no one can be blamed for our loss. All our senses look for a scapegoat. We want to give someone credit for our misery.

PAM W. VREDEVELT, *Empty Arms*

$\mathcal{I}$ cannot forgive my friends for dying: I do not find these vanishing acts of theirs at all amusing.

LOGAN PEARSALL SMITH

I pray that God will at least grant me the favor of being the next to die. I cannot mourn anyone else.

GORDON LIVINGSTON

I can bear to die—I cannot bear to leave her—Oh, Brown, I have coals of fire in my breast. It surprises me that the human heart is capable of containing and bearing so much misery.

JOHN KEATS, letter to Charles Brown

*W*orking at the hospital one soon learned death is not reserved for the aged, nor is it fair in the type of illness it wishes on its victims. I don't believe I ever reached the "Why me" stage. I saw too many without a reason why.

LOUISE, quoted by ELISABETH KÜBLER-ROSS

*W*e must not expect simple answers to far-reaching questions. However far our gaze penetrates, there are always heights which block our vision.

ALFRED NORTH WHITEHEAD

I do not know why God allowed this tragedy. But I believe He is weeping too. He does not take pleasure in our suffering. When we grieve, He grieves.

PASTOR DEAN HONNETTE

$\mathcal{I}$ stop in this moment of stillness, and I know deep inside that the battle is not mine to win. It's beyond me. It's very complicated. I realize most of all that you did not send this trouble. It is part of the evil in our imperfect world. O dear Lord, direct my energies as a parent, and don't let me crumble.

CHARLOTTE AGELSPERGER, *When Your Child Hurts*

$\mathcal{T}$he hardest part of faith is the last half hour.

DAVID WILKERSON

$\mathcal{A}$bsence infects the air
And it is everywhere.
How can I shake off woe,
On what bed lay me down without you?

What healing sacrament
What ritual invent
And quietly perform
To bring life back and make it warm?

Another day a letter
Might tell you I am better,
The invalid has taken
Some food, is less forlorn and shaken.

But for today it's true
That I can hardly draw
A solitary breath
That does not hurt me like a little death.

MAY SARTON, *Halfway To Silence*

He touched his heart but it did not beat, nor did he lift his eyes again. When Gilgamesh touched his heart it did not beat. So Gilgamesh laid a veil, as one veils the bride, over his friend. He began to rage like a lion, like a lioness robbed of her whelps. This way and that he paced round the bed, he tore out his hair and strewed it around. He dragged off his splendid robes and flung them down as though they were abominations…. Gilgamesh lamented; seven days and seven nights he wept for Enkidu, until the worm fastened on him. Only then he gave him up to the earth….

EPIC OF GILGAMESH, story of the 3rd millennium B.C.

Now is my misery full, and namelessly
it fills me. I am stark, as the stone's
inside is stark.
Hard as I am, I know one thing:
You grew—
… and grew
in order to stand forth
as too great pain
quite beyond my heart's grasping.
Now you are lying straight across my lap,
now I can no longer
give you birth.

RAINER MARIA RILKE, *Pieta, The Life of the Virgin Mary*

Take pity on me, Yahweh,
    I am in trouble now.
Grief wastes away my eye,
    my throat, my inmost parts.
For my life is worn out with sorrow,
    my years with sighs;
my strength yields under misery,
    my bones are wasting away.
To every one of my oppressors
    I am contemptible,
loathsome to my neighbours,
    to my friends a thing of fear.

PSALM 31:9-11, *The Jerusalem Bible*

I was just as crazy as you can be and still be at large.
I didn't have any really normal minutes during those two
years. It wasn't just grief. It was total confusion. I was nutty....

HELEN HAYES, quoted by LYNN CAINE

God strengthen me to bear myself,
That heaviest weight of all to bear,
Inalienable weight of care.

CHRISTINA ROSSETTI

My doctor was like a priest to me during times when I felt guilty in a period of mourning. "If you had been able to act differently then, you would have acted differently," she would say. It took me a long time to realize that it is simply not in our power to play out our lives in perfect ways.

ANN KAISER STEARNS, *Living Through Personal Crisis*

Lord.... Please recognize our panic as a prayer.

KIT KUPERSTOCK

No one ever told me that grief felt so like fear. I am not afraid, but the sensation is like being afraid. The same fluttering in the stomach, the same restlessness, the yawning. I keep on swallowing.

C. S. LEWIS, *A Grief Observed*

I didn't realize that it was such a physical thing.... A death—especially the sudden death of a loved one—is a violent act on your body. I felt very much as if I'd been hit by a plank around the shoulders and chest. My head felt heavy. It was a stunning experience.

MARLO THOMAS, referring to the death of her father, Danny Thomas

Grief is what the soul feels when it is wounded, as pain is what the body feels.

MATTHEW CALKINS

*Grief is as varied as fish in the river,
sometimes small and visible in shallows,
sometimes large and mired in the bottom,
and everything in between.*

NEAL BOWERS

*Sometimes, Davie, laughter is a kind of crying when
grieving has left you exhausted and your tears are spent.
We just stood in the hallway holding each other and
laughing.... We felt too bad to risk our tears again.*

MARIE ROTHENBERG and MEL WHITE, *David*

*He disliked emotion, not because he felt lightly, but
because he felt deeply.*

JOHN BUCHAN

*We must not assume that a person is not suffering intense
sorrow simply because he is not showing it. Instead, we must
develop a feeling of empathy for that person so that we can
truly say we are sorry for him in his loss.*

JANE BURGESS KOHN, *The Widower*

*Believe me, every man has his secret sorrows, which
the world knows not; and oftentimes we call a man cold
when he is only sad.*

HENRY WADSWORTH LONGFELLOW

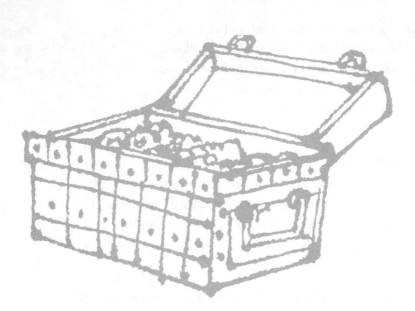

$\mathscr{S}$orrow is like a precious treasure, shown only to friends.

AFRICAN PROVERB

$\mathscr{T}$hough I kept a space of privacy between me and others, I hungered for the intimate, tender support system so easily available to the children. A widower needs a wholly receiving audience for his endless ramblings of fear and sorrow. As much as a child he needs physical contact to comfort his tears and counteract his aloneness. The subtraction of his wife alters his identity, and he needs his self-esteem restored. He needs to sense an escape route out of anxiety and pain. He needs somebody entirely focused on him. The bereaved who have such a person do recover faster.

RICHARD MERYMAN, *Hope: A Loss Survived*

I knew. He knew. He knew that I knew. I knew that he knew that I knew…. The knowledge was too wounding, too burning, too enormously devastating to touch with words or even looks.

LYNN CAINE, *Widow*

I sometimes hold it half a sin
    To put in words the grief I feel;
    For words, like Nature, half reveal
And half conceal the Soul within.

ALFRED, LORD TENNYSON

*I*t is such a secret place, the land of tears.

ANTOINE DE SAINT-EXUPÉRY, *The Little Prince*

I could lie down like a tired child,
And weep away the life of care
Which I have borne and yet must bear,
Till death like sleep might shed on me.

PERCY BYSSHE SHELLEY

*S*orrow makes us all children again.

RALPH WALDO EMERSON

*G*o ahead and let yourself cry. Let somebody hold and support you. When you do, you'll find that a lot of your tiredness and lack of energy will start to lift.

STEPHANIE MATTHEWS SIMONTON, *The Healing Family*

The sorrow which has no vent in tears may make other organs weep.

HENRY MAUDSLEY

He said, "You have to tell such people to lay off clichés about boys not crying. I told my kids, 'It's rough on us losing Mother; it really hurts a lot.' I cry with my children and tell my eighteen-year-old son that it takes a man to cry."

WILLARD K. KOHN, *The Widower*

From a physiological view, when there is emotional stress, gastric secretion increases. Crying not only helps relieve tension but aids in the excretion of lysozyme, which reduces the concentration of gastric juices. A result is a lower incidence of duodenal ulcers in females (six to eight times less frequent in females than in males).... You do not need statistics or clinical cases to demonstrate a truth known to many of us: whatever your age or sex, you simply feel better after a good cry.

EARL A. GROLLMAN, *Talking About Death*

The funeral for Richard, my oldest brother, was a time of bonding for all of us remaining. There were nine kids in my family. Richard was the one who kept in touch with everyone and took the time to visit no matter how far away we moved from our Iowa roots. It makes sense that even in his death, he would strengthen our family ties. Some of my siblings had been feuding, but out of respect for Richard, they came together at the funeral. And we had so much fun together, as humor is a great stress-reliever too!

CHRIS McCANN

Funerals are the rituals we create to help us face the reality of death, to give us a way of expressing our response to that reality with other persons....One funeral I attended was full of the music that the dead person had loved in life. In perfect counterpoint to the music came the rhythms of his loving aunt's sobbing, the outpouring of her heart in the midst of family and friends who could share her sorrow. It was perfectly appropriate to the reality of life and loss ...

ALLA BOZARTH-CAMPBELL, PH.D., *Life is Goodbye Life is Hello*

I can't imagine anything but music that could have brought about this alchemy. Maybe it's because music is about as physical as it gets: your essential rhythm is your heartbeat; your essential sound, the breath. We're walking temples of noise, and when you add tender hearts to this mix, it somehow lets us meet in places we couldn't get to any other way.

ANNE LAMOTT, *Traveling Mercies*

In regard to these kinds of losses, nothing hurts more than not being given the opportunities to express pent-up feelings and emotions, not being able to submit to the pain ... Nothing hurts more than the deep fear that deceased sons and daughters are being forgotten because no one ever talks to them again.

RONALD J. KNAPP, *Beyond Endurance: When A Child Dies*

*G*ive sorrow words; the grief that does not speak
Whispers the oe'r-fraught heart, and bids it break.

WILLIAM SHAKESPEARE, *Macbeth*

From then on I lived at Viareggio, finding courage from the radiance of Eleanora's eyes. She used to rock me in her arms, consoling my pain, but not only consoling, for she seemed to take my sorrow to her own breast, and I realized that if I had not been able to bear the society of other people, it was because they all played the comedy of trying to cheer me with forgetfulness. Whereas Eleanora said:

"Tell me about Dierdre and Patrick," and made me repeat to her all their little sayings and ways, and show her their photos, which she kissed and cried over. She never said, "Cease to grieve," but she grieved with me, and, for the first time since their death, I felt I was not alone.

ISADORE DUNCAN, *My Life*

Lucas is now frozen forever at age 6½. As I grow older will it become harder to picture him as he would be then? Will the passage of time give me some relief from the senseless and demeaning jealousy I feel toward all fathers with healthy sons? What I miss most are two things: the unalloyed admiration I received from him and the feelings of love that he evoked in me. Being his father was the thing I was best at; I find it paralyzingly hard to go on without it.

GORDON LIVINGSTON

Four ducks on a pond,
A grass-bank beyond,
A blue sky of spring,
White clouds on the wing:
What a little thing
To remember for years—
To remember with tears!

WILLIAM ALLINGHAM

Grief fills the room up of my absent child,
Lies in his bed, walks up and down with me,
Puts on his pretty looks, repeats his words,
Remembers me of all his gracious parts,
Stuffs out his vacant garments with his form:
Then have a reason to be fond of grief.

WILLIAM SHAKESPEARE, *King John*

*S*adness, as actually existing, causes pleasure, since it brings to mind that which is loved, the absence of which causes sadness; and yet the mere thought of it gives pleasure.

St. Thomas Aquinas

*T*he death of any familiar person—the death, even, of a dog or cat—whether loved or not leaves an emptiness. The great tree goes down and leaves an empty place against the sky. If the person is deeply loved and deeply familiar the void seems greater than all the world remaining.... But grief is a form of love—the longing for the dear face, the warm hand. It is the remembered reality of the beloved that calls it forth. For an instant she is *there*, and the void denied.

Sheldon Vanauken, *A Severe Mercy*

*G*rief carries its own anesthesia. It gets you over a lot.

Mrs. Lyndon Johnson, Comment made after the death of her husband

*M*ourning.... You seem to be filled with it. Always. In a sense, like a pregnancy. But... pregnancy imparts a sense of doing something even while inactive, [whereas] mourning bequeaths a sense of futility and meaninglessness in the midst of activity.... My everydayness has snapped and I am in quarantine from the world. Want nothing from it, have nothing to give to it. When things get too bad, the whole world is lost to you, the world and the people in it.... Some days I can look at her photograph and the image revives me, reinforces her for me. On other days, I gaze at her and am blinded with tears. Newly bereft....

Toby Talbot, *A Book About My Mother*

It's been more than a year since my mom passed away and suddenly I am grieving like never before. What is it about grief—it plays hide-and-seek. It pops up like a Jack-in-the-box and wraps its arms around you, squeezing so tightly sometimes that it takes your breath away.

KATHLEEN FARADAY

Sometimes in life, our spirits are nearly gone ...
sometimes we feel so crushed and broken and
      overwhelmed ...
that we do not even see where we are going.
We are just out there walking to keep the
      heart beating ...
      and the circulation moving.
but ... if that is all we can do ...
      and we are doing it ...
that is still being faithful ... not quitting...
giving it our best.

ANN KIEMEL, *I'm Running to Win*

We survivors, we who are left behind, know the frustration of helplessness. We carry on because it does not help if we don't. We function, not out of strength, but in the absence of any alternative.

SAMANTHA MOONEY, *A Snowflake In My Hand*

I had not known that the body bore so much,
That so bereaved it still would walk and thrive:
I had not known that, with no sense of touch,
An individual could stay alive.

WITTER BYNNER, *Take Away the Darkness*

*H*ere I stand. I can do no other. God help me. Amen.

MARTIN LUTHER

I sit here in this big house by myself trying to sew but what good is sewing gon do? What good is anything? Being alive begin to seem like a awful strain.

ALICE WALKER, *The Color Purple*

*I*n times like these of such intense physical pain, confusion and doubt, one must simply decide and do, decide and do—and laugh a bit amidst the consequences.

TIM HANSEL, *You Gotta Keep Dancin'*

I've developed a new philosophy—I only dread one day at a time.

CHARLES M. SCHULZ, *Peanuts*

LAMENT

Listen, Children:
Your father is dead:
From his old coats
I'll make you little jackets;
I'll make you little trousers
From his old pants.
There'll be in his pockets
Things he used to put there,
Keys and pennies
Covered with tobacco;
Dan shall have the pennies
To save in his bank;
Anne shall have the keys
To make pretty noise with.
Life must go on.
And the dead be forgotten;
Life must go on,
Though good men die;
Anne, eat your breakfast;
Dan, take your medicine;
Life must go on;
I forget just why.

EDNA ST. VINCENT MILLAY, *Second April*

One aspect of deep grief is loss of the imagination. One cannot imagine a time when one is not in pain…. How many times have I sabotaged myself by leaping ahead of my own healing process, trying so desperately to "feel better" that I make myself feel even worse because I have added to my primary pain the new complication of failure! In cheating myself of the necessary time to feel bad I have cheated myself of the only process that could really heal me.

Ultimately, the only way to get through something is to get *through* it—not over, under, or around it, but all the way through it. And it takes as long as it takes.

ALLA BOZARTH-CAMPBELL, PH.D., *Life is Goodbye Life is Hello*

Penny said, "You've seed how things goes in the world o' men. You've knowed men to be low-down and mean. You've seed ol' Death at his tricks. You've messed around with ol' Starvation. Ever' man wants life to be a fine thing, and easy. 'Tis fine, boy, powerful fine, but 'tain't easy. Life knocks a man down and he gits up and it knocks him down agin. I've been uneasy all my life."

MARLORIE KINNAN RAWLINGS, *The Yearling*

Far from disassociating himself from our pain, the God of love, peace, hope and joy meets us right there at the very point of our hurt…. He calls us to face our own pain; he calls us to face the reality of our own unhappiness; he calls us to enter into our own suffering and to embrace the pain of others because it is there that we meet the one who has embraced the agony of the whole world in his death on the cross.

THE REV. KENNETH B. SWANSON, PH.D.

*L*ife is an onion
and one peels it crying.

FRENCH PROVERB

*H*elp me to realize that I am
not the only person who finds
it difficult to start the day.

F. TOPPING

And I was having to bear the unbearable. If I must bear it, I would bear it—find the whole meaning of it, taste the whole of it.... I would not run away from grief; I would not try to hold on to it when—if, unbelievably—it passed.

SHELDON VANAUKEN, *A Severe Mercy*

Dearest friend, please believe that I understand the pain in your heart, the void in your gut, the cut-off feeling, the many things you never told her and the pain of knowing you never will. The agony of death, at this moment, for you is unbearable, but please, be patient. Time will soothe your pain.

With love and deep hope that the time will pass quickly for you ...

TERI, quoted by DR. ROBERTA TEMES

SMALL PRAYER

Change, move, dead clock, that this fresh day
May break with dazzling light to these sick eyes.
Burn, glare, old sun, so long unseen,
That time may find its sand again, and cleanse
Whatever it is that a wound remembers
After the healing ends.

WELDON KEES

In three words I can sum up everything I've learned about life. It goes on.

ROBERT FROST

$\mathcal{A}$ lot of people look in the wrong places for healing. To find closure and direction, they may turn to such things as palm readers and psychics who have the potential to lead them in even more damaging directions. But I found that if you stick it out, and if you seek God, you will eventually find peace and new reasons to go on.

KIM WALKER who lost a 5-year old daughter

$\mathcal{M}$ost people though, manage to make their way through the painful stages of grief and eventually regain their emotional balance. What they need desperately are caring friends and relatives who allow them to grieve in their own way, at their own pace and who, above all, will not insist that they act like their "old selves." For no one who has suffered a terrible loss will ever be her old self again. She may be a different self or even a better self, but she will never regain the identity that was untouched by grief.

SUSAN JACOBY

$\mathcal{T}$hroughout these days Mary had, during these breathing spells, drawn a kind of solace from the recurrent thought: at least I am enduring it. I am aware of what has happened, I am meeting it face to face, I am living through it. There had been, even, a kind of pride, a desolate kind of pleasure, in the feeling: I am carrying a heavier weight than I could have dreamed it possible for a human being to carry, yet I am living through it. It had of course occurred to her that this happens to many people, that it is very common, and she humbled and comforted herself in this thought.

JAMES AGEE, *A Death In The Family*

One of the things I find most astounding is that, though we think of the future life as something perfected, when Christ appeared to his disciples He said, "Come look at my hands," and He invited Thomas to put his finger into the print of the nail. Why did He want to keep the wounds of His humanity? Wasn't it because He wanted to carry back with Him an eternal reminder of the sufferings of those on earth? He carried the marks of suffering so He could continue to understand the needs of those suffering.

DR. PAUL BRAND, hand surgeon quoted in *Where Is God When It Hurts?* by Philip Yancey

Not a day passes over the earth, but men and women of no note do great deeds, speak great words and suffer noble sorrows.

CHARLES READE

And while we laugh or cry for different reasons,
The sound of happiness is much the same everywhere.
And tears, wept for whatever reason,
Always tast of salt.

MARILEE ZDENEK

Here is to the world that goes round on wheels.
Death is a thing that all man feels.
If living was a thing that money could buy,
The rich would live and the poor would die.

ANONYMOUS

*D*on't you remember sweet Alice, Ben Bolt—
   Sweet Alice whose hair was so brown,
Who wept with delight when you gave her a smile,
   And trembled with fear at your frown?

In the old churchyard in the valley, Ben Bolt,
   In a corner obscure and alone,
They have fitted a slab of the granite so gray
   And Alice lies under the stone.

And don't you remember the school, Ben Bolt,
   With the master so cruel and grim,
And the shaded nook in the running brook
   Where the children went to swim?

Grass grows on the master's grave, Ben Bolt,
   The spring of the brook is dry.
And of all the boys who were schoolmates then
   There are only you and I.

THOMAS DUNN ENGLISH

*T*here is time for everything.
   and a season for every activity under heaven:
   a time to be born and a time to die,
   a time to plant and a time to uproot,
   a time to kill and a time to heal,
   a time to tear down and a time to build,
   a time to weep and a time to laugh,
   a time to mourn and a time to dance…

ECCLESIASTES 3:1-4, *NIV*

$\mathcal{D}$eath is clearly no failure.

BARBARA GENEST

$\mathcal{N}$umberless are the world's wonders, but none more
wonderful than man ...
... from every wind
He has made himself secure—from all but one:
In the last wind of death he cannot stand.

SOPHICLES

$\mathcal{D}$eath knocks, as we know, at the door of the cottage
and of the castle.

ZULEIKA DOBSON

The man can neither make, nor retain, one moment of time; it all comes to him by pure gift; he might as well regard the sun and moon as his chattels.

C. S. Lewis, *The Screwtape Letters*

If none can 'scape Death's dreadful dart;
   If rich and poor his beck obey;
If strong, if wise, if all do smart,
   Then I to 'scape shall have no way:
Then grant me grace, O God! that I
My life may mend, since I must die.

Robert Southwell

CHAPTER THREE

Letting go

Letting go

It was my last day of work and Rita's last week of life. For two months, since my new job offer, I had prepared myself to leave this hospital. For three months, since her diagnosis, Rita had prepared herself to leave this life.

I studied her face to find the words for goodbye. She had become one of those graced individuals who acquire a certain calmness and wisdom as death becomes a more present reality. I think I needed her blessing more than she needed mine.

"Jill," Rita said with a voice that seemed both young and old, "I wanted to give you a goodbye present but couldn't find anyone to go out and buy it. Please open my top drawer and take out ten dollars."

"Oh, Rita, I don't need your money to know that you appreciate and care about me."

Rita became stern. "Please, Jill. Take the money and buy a new pair of socks for yourself and think of me when you wear them."

I love my new socks.

CHAPTER THREE is about saying goodbye. Goodbye to life and goodbye to each other. But how does one get such a sweet spirit of acceptance that lets go and kisses goodbye? Chapter Three seeks to explain this mystery of peace that comes after torment; strength that comes after struggle; and wisdom that comes after confusion.
C. S. Lewis, Madeleine L'Engle, Annie Dillard, and many others offer you glimpses into the hope and meaning they have found. As you read their thoughts, you will be challenged and inspired to open your own mind and heart to find for yourself that peace that surpasses understanding and enables you to let go.

Things have fallen apart, haven't they; that realization must come to all of us, it is a prerequisite to remedy.

GEORGE JACKSON, Soledad prisoner, *Soledad Brother: The Prison Letters of George Jackson*

In his last exhausting fight for life, only a few hours before he went to heaven, he declared, "Something good has got to come out of this."

CHARLOTTE ADELSPERGER, *When Your Child Hurts*

We must kick the darkness 'til it bleeds daylight.

BRUCE COCHBURN, from the song, "Lovers in a Dangerous Time"

I am a more sensitive person, a more effective pastor, a more sympathetic counselor because of Aaron's life and death than I would ever have been without it. And I would give up all of those gains in a second if I could have my son back. If I could choose, I would forego all the spiritual growth and depth which has come my way because of our experiences, and be what I was fifteen years ago, an average rabbi, an indifferent counselor, helping some people and unable to help others, and the father of a bright, happy boy. But I cannot choose.

RABBI HAROLD KUSHNER, referring to the death of his firstborn, *When Bad Things Happen To Good People*

The world breaks everyone, and afterward many are strong at the broken places.

ERNEST HEMINGWAY, *A Farewell To Arms*

I saw a very real change take place in Rico, particularly during the last six months when it became apparent to him that he was fighting a losing battle. It was like a calmness enveloped him. He wasn't what you would call moody, but more contemplative. He seemed to set aside boyish things and boyish behavior.... I think he displayed more control and wisdom during those last six months than most people do in a lifetime. He became my main support during that time.

RONALD J. KNAPP, quoting a mother whose 12-year-old died of Ewing's tumor

I do not believe that sheer suffering teaches. If suffering alone taught, all the world would be wise, since everyone suffers. To suffering must be added mourning, understanding, patience, love, openness and willingness to remain vulnerable.

ANNE MORROW LINDBERGH

It is good for thee to dwell deep, that thou mayest feel and understand the spirits of people.

JOHN WOOLMAN

My mother had always been a tortured soul. When she was dying, true to form, she refused all painkillers. But I think it was out of this suffering that spiritual changes took place. I won't speak for others, but for me, no matter how painful a death is, I would never help a person end their life. Why? Because I saw my mother learn profound lessons in her last days. I saw it and I felt it. While in soul-wrenching pain, she went through a spiritual transformation, though she could barely communicate. Then, using all her strength, she gave me the best gift ever—she told me that she loved me, something she had never told me before.

TERESA WOLFE

The self must be destroyed, brought down to nothing, in order for self-transcendence to begin. Then the self can begin to relate to powers beyond itself. It has to thrash around in its finitude, it has to "die," in order to question that finitude, in order to see beyond it.

ERNEST BECKER, *The Denial of Death*

The single saying of Jesus which the Bible records more often than any other (four times) expresses a paradoxical truth: "Whoever finds his life will lose it, and whoever loses his life for my sake will find it." Sometimes seeming tragedies, like pain and suffering, can nudge us along the path to "losing our lives…"

PHILIP YANCEY, *Where Is God When It Hurts?*

*H*ow does one become a butterfly?"
She asked pensively.

"You must want to fly so much
that you are willing to give
up being a caterpillar."

"You mean to *die*?" asked Yellow....
"Yes and No," he answered.
"What *looks* like you will die
But what's *really* you will still live."

TRINA PAULUS, *Hope for the Flowers*

$\mathscr{S}$elf surrender... takes away fear of death because you have already died, you have died to you as the center of you.

CURTIS JONES, *How Come We're Alive?*

$\mathscr{O}$ Lord, by all thy dealings with us, whether of joy or pain, of light or darkness, let us be brought to thee. Let us value no treatment of thy grace simply because it makes us happy or because it makes us sad, because it give us or denies us what we want; but may all that thou sendest us bring us to thee, knowing thy perfectness, we may be sure in every disappointment that thou art still loving us, and in every darkness that thou art still enlightening us, and in every enforced idleness that thou art still using us; yea, in every death thou art still giving us life, as in his death thou didst give life to thy Son, our Saviour, Jesus Christ. Amen.

PHILLIPS BROOKS, "A Prayer For All Seasons"

$\mathscr{P}$ain casts us out of ourselves to seek healing and comfort from our friends and family and, at our deepest psychic and spiritual levels, pain casts us outside of ourselves to seek comfort and healing of God.

THE REV. KENNETH B. SWANSON, PH.D.

$\mathscr{T}$he Lord is close to the brokenhearted
and saves those who are crushed in spirit.

PSALM 34:18, *NIV*

My life is like the faded leaf,
　My harvest dwindled to a husk;
Truly my life is void and brief
　And tedious in the barren dusk;
My life is like a frozen thing,
　No bud nor greenness can I see:
Yet rise it shall,—the sap of Spring;
　O Jesus, rise in me!

Christina Rossetti

Life begins on the other side of despair.

Jean-Paul Sartre

The second before the sun went out we saw a wall of dark shadow come speeding at us. We no sooner saw it than it was upon us, like thunder. It roared up the valley. It slammed our hill and knocked us out. It was the monstrous swift shadow cone of the moon. I have since read that this wave of shadow moves 1,800 miles an hour. Language can give no sense of this sort of speed—1,800 miles an hour. It was 195 miles wide. No end was is sight—you saw only the edge. It rolled at you across the land at 1,800 miles an hour, hauling darkness like plague behind it.…

　Less than two minutes later, when the sun emerged, the trailing edge of the shadow cone sped away. It coursed down our hill and raced eastward over the plain and dropped over the planet's rim in a twinkling. It had clobbered us, and now it roared away. We blinked in the light.

Annie Dillard, observations on the total eclipse at Yakima, Washington, *Teaching A Stone To Talk*

The winter of the soul, in its seeming barrenness, its times of seeming unproductivity, its times of silence and seeming stalemate, is perhaps its most important season. Without it, there is no recovery of freshness and vitality; no bursting forth in springtime splendor.

DWIGHT H. JUDY

Pure water lily how grew you so white
Rising through dark water?

ADA C. PERRY

We see death all around us. Plants, animals, friends, family all die. We know, too, that we will die; but as we witness the glorious rebirth of nature in springtime, we inevitably ask ourselves, is death the ultimate and final end; does it have the last word to say about our life?... We may rationally reject the hope and confidence at the core of our being; it may well be a deception, the last trick, the ultimate deception of the vindictive, cruel and arbitrary universe. But the decisive religious question, perhaps the only religious question that really matters, is whether that hope which is at the center of our personality is cruel deception or whether it is a hint of an explanation, a rumor of angels, the best insight we have into what human life is all about.

ANDREW GREELEY, *Death and Beyond*

The loftiest hope is the surest of being fulfilled.

GEORGE MACDONALD, *The Castle: A Parable*

It is plain that the hope of a future life arises from the
feeling, which exists in the breast of every man, that the
temporal is inadequate to meet and satisfy the demands
of his nature.

IMMANUEL KANT, *Critique of Pure Reason*

I do not recall the time when
I was not conscious of a hunger
    for something
beyond the physical and the material.

MARY SUE TYNES LUNDY

Wear the world like a loose garment.

CHARLES HAYES

Renouncing the honors at which the world aims, I desire
only to know the truth, and to live as well as I can, and, when
I die, to die as well as I can.

PLATO, quoted by Gollancz from *Darkness to Light*

My question, the question that had brought me to the edge of suicide when I was fifty years old, was the simplest question lying in the soul of every human being, from a silly child to the wisest of the elders, the question without which life is impossible; such was the way I felt about the matter. The question is this: What will come of what I do today and tomorrow? What will come of my entire life?

Expressed differently, the question may be: Why should I live? Why should I wish for anything or do anything? Or to put it still differently: Is there any meaning in my life that will not be destroyed by my inevitably approaching death?

No matter what answers a given faith might provide for us, every answer of faith gives infinite meaning to the finite existence of man, meaning that is not destroyed by suffering, deprivation, and death. Therefore, the meaning of life and the possibility of living may be found in faith alone … faith is to answer the questions of a tsar dying in the midst of luxury, an old slave tormented in his labor; an ignorant child, an aged sage, a half-witted old lady, a happy young woman, and a youth consumed by passions …

LEO TOLSTOY, *Confessions*

It is such great news to tell these high school kids that there is more to life. To assure them that they are not just random bits of meaningless molecules, but rather created and loved by God for an eternal existence!

MARV REIF, **Young Life leader**

I don't know who—or what—put the question, I don't know when it was put. I don't remember answering. But at some moment I did answer Yes to Someone—or Something— and from that hour I was certain that existence is meaningful and that, therefore, my life, in self-surrender, had a goal.

DAG HAMMARSKJÖLD, *Markings*

*I*f it is true that there is Someone in charge of the whole mystery of life and death, we can hardly expect to escape a sense of futility and frustration until we begin to see what He is like and what His purposes are.

J.B. PHILLIPS, *Your God Is Too Small*

*S*eek not to understand that thou mayest believe, but believe that thou mayest understand.

ST. AUGUSTINE

*L*ong ago, I asked my parents
    (using other words)
    "Am I of value? Does my life have meaning?"
Then I asked my teachers,
    later, directors and editors,
    husband and friends—
    "Am I of value? Does my life have meaning?"
Then I asked God and God said, "Yes."

MARILEE ZDENEK

*F*or myself, I find some measure of reassurance against the nagging doubt of meaninglessness in the implications of what has been considered by some thinkers as the profoundest, even though unanswerable, question: Why is there something rather than nothing? What this question implies is that there is no necessity of there being a world at all. But precisely because it would have been so easy not to have been, the existence of the world and of my own individual self must have a significance, a meaning that goes beyond the mere fact of its and my own existing.

JACQUES CHORON, *Death and Modern Man*

*I*n 1998, seventy-seven-year-old John Glenn returned to space. Almost immediately, he was overwhelmed with the presence of God. "Looking at the Earth from this vantage point," he told reporters, "looking at this kind of creation and to not believe in God, to me, is impossible."

GARY THOMAS, *Sacred Pathways*

*M*y special place is a small brook in a green glade, a circle of quiet from which there is no visible sign of human beings. There's a natural stone bridge over the brook, and I sit there, dangling my legs and looking through the foliage at the sky reflected in the water, and things slowly come back into perspective. If the insects are biting me—and they usually are; no place is quite perfect—I use the pliable branch of a shadblow tree as a fan. The brook wanders through a tunnel of foliage, and the birds sing more sweetly there than anywhere else; or perhaps it is just that when I am at the brook I have time to be aware of them, and I move slowly into a kind of peace that is marvelous...

MADELEINE L'ENGLE, *A Circle of Quiet*

I looked down the valley of Granite Creek.... The whole course of the stream was visible, from the tickling snowpack through lush forest to the burning plain where it gave up its ghosts. I saw that stream in all phases of its life—as God might see in my life or my country's life—under the aspect of eternity. No trout could have such a view, and I tried to imagine them asking, in some flickering, troutlike way, where their creek began or whether it reached the sea.

JOHN TALLMADGE

At any given moment, life is completely senseless. But viewed over a period, it seems to reveal itself as an organism existing in time, having a purpose, tending in a certain direction.

ALDOUS HUXLEY

My life has been a tapestry between my God and me;
I do not choose the colors, He worketh steadily.
Oftimes He weaveth sorrow, And I, in foolish pride,
Forget He sees the upper and I the underside.
But the dark threads, they're as needful
In the Skillful Weaver's hand
As the threads of gold and silver
In the pattern He has planned.

ANONYMOUS

We would be saved from all kinds of mistakes if we always looked at things in the light of eternity.

WILLIAM BARCLAY

That is what mortals misunderstand. They say of some temporal suffering, "No future bliss can make up for it," not knowing that Heaven, once attained, will work backwards and turn even the agony into a glory.

C.S. LEWIS, *The Great Divorce*

Life must be understood backwards.

SOREN KIERKEGAARD

*N*ow we see but a poor reflection as in a mirror; then we shall see face to face. Now I know in part; then I shall know fully, even as I am fully known.

I Corinthians 13:12, *NIV*

*F*aith is to believe what we do not see, and the reward of this faith is to see what we believe.

St. Augustine

*A*nd I was wondering if you had been to the mountain to look at the valley below? Did you see all the roads tangled down in the valley? Did you know which way to go? Oh the mountain stream runs pure and clear and I wish to my soul I could always be here. But there's a reason for living way down in the valley that only the mountain knows.

Noel Paul Stookey, from the song, "John Henry Bosworth"

*N*either despise nor oppose what thou dost not understand.

WILLIAM PENN

*F*ARTHER ALONG

Tempted and tried, we're oft made to wonder
Why it should be thus all the day long.
While there are others living above us;
Never molested, though in the wrong.

Farther along we'll know all about it;
Farther along we'll understand why.
Cheer up my brothers, live in the sunshine,
We'll understand it all by and by.

SOUTHERN GOSPEL HYMN

*A*nd whether or not it is clear to you, no doubt the universe is unfolding as it should. Therefore be at peace with God....

MAX EHRMANN

*I*ndeed, I am persuaded that there is nothing in the arsenal of medical or psychological technology that equals the power inherent in a simple faith.

ROBERT VENINGA, *A Gift of Hope*

Having faith is a necessary step toward one of two things. Being healed is one of them. Peace of mind, if healing doesn't come, is the other. Either one will suffice.

BRIAN STERNBERG, paralyzed from the neck down due to a trampoline accident

When praying for healing, ask great things of God and expect great things from God. But let us seek for that healing what really matters, the healing of the heart....

ARLO F. NEWELL

It is more important, more thrilling, more satisfying and infinitely more valuable to know the Healer than to be healed.

ANONYMOUS

I noted that the faces of people who have a terminal disease, and who have come to terms with their own impending death have a look that is a marvelous combination of tranquility and incredible power and insight.

MAL WARSHAW

The heart of the wise is in the house of mourning...

ECCLESIASTES 7:4, *NIV*

*Y*ou're going to die," I said to myself. "This is really it and you had better say something definitive, something that will sum up your life."

The necessity to pronounce harassed me because, quite frankly, I could think of nothing to say. And I fretted through the long hours until it occurred to me, in the middle of the night, that I really didn't need to say anything at all. Nobody expected it or even wanted it. Having talked all my life ceaselessly, it seemed likely that if I hadn't said what I'd meant to say by now, it wasn't from lack of trying, and that, in fact, my whole life was what I had to say; my habits of living were my statements....

What else did I dare think about? Not so very much. Nothing profound. I didn't kick against fate. The fact was, I had had a long vigorous life. While I had had my body I had used it, God knows. I was lucky to have had it full of health and effectiveness as long as I had.... I did not say, "Why me?" because the answer was so patently clear: "Why not me?"

AGNES DE MILLE, *Reprieve*

*D*id you think.... That you needed, say, life? Do you think you will keep your life, or anything else you love? But no.... You see creatures die, and you know that you will die. And one day it occurs to you that you must not need life.

ANNIE DILLARD, *Pilgrim At Tinker Creek*

This body is my house—it is not I.
Triumphant in this faith, I live and die.

ANONYMOUS

I don't know what will happen to me …
We've got some difficult days ahead,
But it doesn't matter to me now …
I've been to the mountain top …
Like anybody I'd like to live a long life …
But I'm not concerned about that now.
I just want to do God's will.
And he's allowed me to go up the mountain.
And I've looked over,
And I've seen the Promised Land.

MARTIN LUTHER KING, JR., from a speech delivered
the day before his death

The salmon is still the swimmer in our language....They watched her last valiant fight for life, her struggle to right herself when the gentle stream turned her, and they watched the river force open her gills and draw her slowly downstream, tail first, as she had started to the sea as a fingerling....Mark saw that in Keetah's eyes there were tears.

"It is always the same," she said. "The end of the swimmer is sad."

"But, Keetah, it isn't. The whole life of the swimmer is one of courage and adventure. All of it builds to the climax and the end. When the swimmer dies he has spent himself completely for the end which he has made, and this is not sadness. It is triumph."

MARGARET CRAVEN, *I Heard The Owl Call My Name*

Now, only memory
Brings back the tempests
Made by your reckless will
    Which pressed Life
        itself
    To cry Halt

The reaching and the daring
Were not your doing
    'Twas Nature
    In your
        body
    Too fiercely brewing.

WILLIAM J. RICE

$\mathcal{S}$ome people confuse acceptance with apathy, but there's all the difference in the world. Apathy fails to distinguish between what can and cannot be helped; acceptance makes that distinction. Apathy paralyzes the will-to-action; acceptance frees it by relieving it of impossible burdens.

ARTHUR GORDON, *A Touch Of Wonder*

$\mathcal{H}$ope claims the possibilities of the future, hopelessness recognizes its limits. In the mature person there are feelings of both, but they are kept distinct and separate. There's nothing wrong with hopeless feelings as long as they only limit, but do not contaminate the hope.

WILLIAM LYNCH, *Images of Hope*

FALSE HOPE:

If I permit only optimistic thoughts
If I allow only positive feelings
If I dream only possibility dreams
Then I miss what has been
And elude what might be.

TRUE HOPE:

If I face both good and evil
If I feel both fear and calm
If I live in the world as it is
Then I stand on what has been
And accept what may be.

Adapted from DAVID AUGSBURGER, *When Enough is Enough*

O God, give us serenity to accept what cannot be changed; courage to change what should be changed, and wisdom to distinguish the one from the other.

REINHOLD NIEBUHR

*S*uffer us not to mock ourselves with falsehood
Teach us to care and not to care
Teach us to sit still
Even among these rocks,
Our peace in His will
And even among these rocks
Sister, mother
And spirit of the river, spirit of the sea,
Suffer me not to be separated

And let my cry come unto Thee.

T. S. ELIOT, from the poem, "Ash Wednesday"

*B*ut the painting selected by the judges for the first prize was very different from all the others. It depicted the height of a raging storm. Trees bent low under lashing wind and driving rain. Lightning zigzagged across a lowering threatening sky. In the center of the fury the artist had painted a bird's nest in the crotch of a gigantic tree. There a mother bird spread her wings over her little brood, waiting serene and unruffled until the storm would pass. The painting was entitled very simply, Peace.

CATHERINE MARSHALL, *The Helper*

My life flows on
An endless song
Above earth's lamentation
I hear the real though far-off hymn
That hails a new creation.

No storm can shake
My inmost calm
While to that Rock I'm clinging.
Since love is Lord of heaven and earth
How can I keep from singing?

FOLK SONG

Those who have the strength and the love to sit with a dying patient in the *silence that goes beyond words* will know that this moment is neither frightening nor painful, but a peaceful cessation of the functioning of the body. Watching a peaceful death of a human being reminds us of a falling star; one of the million lights in a vast sky that flares up for a brief moment only to disappear into the endless night forever.

ELISABETH KÜBLER-ROSS, *On Death and Dying*

I came in with Halley's Comet in 1835. It is coming again next year, and I expect to go out with it. It will be the greatest disappointment of my life if I don't go out with Halley's Comet. The Almighty has said, no doubt: "Now here are these two unaccountable freaks; they came in together, they must go out together."

MARK TWAIN, died April 21, 1910, the day after the perihelion of Halley's Comet

And in Thy book they were all written,
The days that were ordained for me,
When as yet there was not one of them.

PSALM 139:16, *New American Standard Bible*

*O*ne day I was alone with her. She was so sick and weak.
I knew I had to do it soon. But how to do it? That was the
question! How do I prepare a four-year-old child to die? She
was lying on her bed in her room. I sat down next to her and
said, "Cindy, I have something I want to tell you." She turned
and looked at me with tears in her eyes. I said, "I know you
have been feeling bad for quite a few months now. You can't
play anymore; you can't go to nursery school anymore; you
can't go to Sunday school anymore; you can't dance anymore.
But there is a real special place you can go and pretty soon
you will be going there. Do you know where that place is,
Cindy?" She thought for a moment, then said "Heaven?" I said,
"That's right!" Then I told her about all the people she would
see there, all her little friends, and her grandparents. "They
will be waiting for you," I told her. She had been listening very
intently. Then, forcing back my own tears, I said, "But before
you go to heaven, Cindy, you first have to die!" She just looked
at me and said, "Oh, Mommy, I know that!" And I got the
feeling she really did know and was now so glad that I knew
too! It was no longer a secret that she had to keep. She seemed
so relieved that she no longer had to protect me.

I saw a definite change in her after that. She became less
agitated and seemed more comfortable. We talked a lot about
heaven and about what she would shortly experience. She died
four days later, and I am so glad now that I found the strength
to do what I did. She seemed to experience a freedom upon
discovering that at last I knew what she had apparently known
for a long time.

RONALD J. KNAPP, quoting the mother of a four-year-old child
with leukemia

The greatest act of personal faith is to die because it's something you have to do yourself—no one can do it for you. You have to let go and trust that God will be there to catch you. It's also your last chance to humble yourself and admit your need for Him to be there on the other side.

HUGH PERRY

MY SOUL AND I

As treading some long corridor,
    My soul and I together go;
Each day unlock another door
    To a new room we did not know.

And every night the darkness hides
    My soul from me awhile—but then
No fear nor loneliness abides;
    Hand clasped in hand, we wake again.

So when my soul and I, at last,
    Shall find but one dim portal more,
Shall we remembering all the past,
    Yet fear to try that other door?

CHARLES BUXTON GOING

We have been so long accustomed to the hypothesis of your being taken away from us, especially during the past ten months, that the thought that this may be your last illness conveys no very sudden shock. You are old enough, you've given your message to the world in many ways and will not be forgotten; you are here left alone, and on the other side, let us hope and pray, dear, dear old Mother is waiting for you to join her. If you go, it will not be an inharmonious thing.... It is so much like the act of bidding an ordinary good night. Good night, my sacred old Father! If I don't see you again—Farewell! a blessed farewell!

WILLIAM JAMES, letter to his father, Henry James, Sr., during the latter's final illness

Death is a night that lies between two days—the day of life on earth and the day of eternal life in the world to come.

MAURICE LAMM, *The Jewish Way In Death And Mourning*

Praise day at night and life at the end.

GEORGE HERBERT

Each day is a little life; every waking and rising a little birth, every fresh morning a little youth, every going to rest and sleep a little death.

ARTHUR SCHOPENHAUER

$\mathcal{I}$ have never wanted any released friend of mine restored to life since I reached manhood. I felt in this way when Susy passed away; and later my wife, and later Mr. Rogers. When Clara met me at the station in New York and told me Mr. Rogers had died suddenly that morning, my thought was, Oh, favorite of fortune—fortunate all his long and lovely life—fortunate to his latest moment! The reporters said there were tears of sorrow in my eyes. True—but they were for *me*, not for him. He had suffered no loss.

MARK TWAIN, *The Autobiography of Mark Twain*

$\mathcal{D}$one crossed every river,
Done reached this one;
Now I know my crossin's done.
Hallelujah, Lord, your rest feel good.
Hallelujah, Lord, your rest feel good.

OWEN DOBSON, *The Harlem Book of the Dead*

$\mathcal{S}$leep on in thy beauty,
    Thou sweet angel child,
By sorrow unslighted,
    By sin undefined.
Like the dove to the ark,
    Thou hast flown to the rest,
From the wild sea of strife,
    To the home of the blest.

Mourning Card of James S. Pilling, dead at age 8, 1889

I leave the world without a tear
Save for the friends I hold so dear
To heal their sorrows Lord descend
And to the friendless prove a friend

Gravestone in memory of Mary A. Brown, 1827

He has outsoared the shadow of our night;
Envy and calumny and hate and pain,
And that unrest which men miscall delight
Can touch him not and torture not again;
From the contagion of the world's slow strain
He is secure, and now can never mourn
A heart grown cold, a head grown grey in vain.

PERCY BYSSHE SHELLEY

Death is in my sight today
As when a man desires to see home
When he has spent many years in captivity.

The Man Who Was Tired of Life, C. 1990 B.C.

I saw battle-corpses, myriads of them,
and the white skeletons of young men, I saw them;
I saw the debris and debris of all the slain soldiers of the war,
But I saw they were not as was thought:
They themselves were fully at rest, they suffer'd not;
The living remain'd and suffer'd, the mother suffer'd,
And the wife and the child and the musing comrade suffer'd,
And the armies that remain'd suffer'd.

WALT WHITMAN, from "When Lilacs Last in the Dooryard Bloom'd"

Ah! Vanitas vanitatum! Which of us is happy in this world? Which of us has his desire? Or, having it, is satisfied?—Come, children, let us shut up the box and the puppets, for our play is played out.

WILLIAM MAKEPEACE THACKERAY

No doubt it is hard to die, but it is sweet to think that we shall not live for ever, and that a better life will put an end to the sorrows of this world. If we had the offer of immortality here below, who would accept the sorrowful gift?

JEAN-JACQUES ROUSSEAU, *Emile*

The modern philosophers had told me again and again that I was in the right place, and I had still felt depressed even in acquiescence. But I had heard that I was in the wrong place, and my soul sang for joy, like a bird in spring.

G.K. CHESTERTON, *Orthodoxy*

While we are aspiring towards our true country, we be pilgrims on earth.

JOHN CALVIN

Dear God, thank you for this wonderful present of being on earth before we go to heaven.

PRAYER BY ALI RABIDEAU, 7 years old

We have not always been or will not always be purely temporal creatures…. Not only are we harried by time, we seem unable, despite a thousand generations, even to get used to it. We are always amazed at it—how fast it goes, how slowly it goes, how much of it is gone. Where, we cry, has the time gone? We aren't adapted to it, not at home in it. If that is so, it may appear as a proof, or at least a powerful suggestion, that eternity exists and is our home….

SHELDON VANAUKEN

In this mode of perception, biological death can be understood as the annihilation of the final set of barriers between man and God, and as the Supreme achievement of transcendence. Time does not matter here: "Before Abraham was," said Jesus, "I Am."

SANDOL STODDARD, *The Hospice Movement*

One gets glimpses, even in our country, of that which is ageless—heavy thought in the face of an infant, and frolic childhood in that of a very old man.

C.S. LEWIS, *The Great Divorce*

When my mother passed, my father said her face softened and she looked like she did when she was 18, about forty years ago when he had first met her.

EMILY RAMPIN

*H*ere lies a poor woman who was always tired,
She lived in a house where help wasn't hired:
Her last words on earth were: "Dear friends, I am going
To where there's no cooking, or washing, or sewing—
Don't mourn for me now, don't mourn for me never,
I am going to do nothing for ever and ever."

ANONYMOUS

*N*o one knows whether death, which men in their fear apprehend to be the greatest evil, may not be the greatest good.

PLATO, *Apology*

*C*hildren are always concerned that their parents aren't treating them fairly. I try to be as fair as possible with my two, but sometimes I make decisions on their behalf that call their indignations into full force. I tell them that I, as their old and wise parent, am making the very best call for them with the given circumstances. I tell them that they have to trust me on this, even though things may look unfair to their young, inexperienced minds. Needless to say, this explanation does not satisfy them in the least. But maybe, when they're older, and life seems to treat them unfairly, it may cross their minds that God above has made a move that they can't possibly understand with their limited perspective, but, in terms of eternity, it's for their best.

GAIL PERRY JOHNSTON

A dialogue between two infants in the womb concerning the state of this world, might handsomely illustrate our ignorance of the next.

SIR THOMAS BROWNE

*L*ife is a great surprise. I do not see why death should not be an even greater one.

VLADIMIR NABOKOV

*T*he sight of stars always sets me dreaming just as naively as those dots on a map set me dreaming of towns and villages. Why should those points of light in the firmament, I wonder, be less accessible than the dark ones on the map of France? We take a train to go to Tarascon or Rouen, and we take death to go to a star.

VINCENT VAN GOGH, *referring to his painting, "The Starry Night"*

*D*eath is only a horizon; and a horizon is nothing save the limit of our sight.

ROSSITER WORTHINGTON RAYMOND

*S*till around the corner there may wait
A new road, or a secret gate.

J.R.R. TOLKIEN

I never saw a Moor—
I never saw the Sea—
Yet know I how the Heather looks
And what a Billow be.

I never spoke with God
Nor visited in Heaven—
Yet certain am I of the spot
As if the Checks were given

EMILY DICKINSON

*W*hen the great chemist, Sir Faraday, was on his deathbed,
some journalists questioned him as to his speculations
concerning the soul and death. "Speculations!" said the dying
man in astonishment, "I know nothing about speculations,
I am resting on certainties."

MRS. CHARLES E. COWMAN

*M*y life is drawing to a close. I know that, I feel it.
But I also feel every day that is left to me how my earthly
life is already in touch with a new, infinite, unknown but
fast approaching future life, the anticipation of which sets
my soul trembling with rapture, and my mind glowing,
and my heart weeping with joy."

FYODOR DOSTOEVSKY, *The Brothers Karamazov*

*W*ill the circle be unbroken?
By and by, Lord, by and by
There's a better home a waitin'
In the sky, Lord, in the sky.

FOLK SONG

I saw eternity the other night
Like a great ring of pure and endless light.

HENRY VAUGHAN, *The World*

*O*n earth the broken arcs;
in heaven, a perfect round.

ROBERT BROWNING

$\mathscr{I}$ was never afraid of Hell, nor never grew pale at the description of that place; I have so fixed my contemplations on heaven, that I have almost forgot the Idea of Hell, and am afraid rather to lose the Joys of the one, than endure the misery of the other....

SIR THOMAS BROWNE, *Religio Medici*

$\mathscr{C}$ome now, thou greatest of feasts on the journey
   to freedom eternal;
Death, cast aside all the burdensome chains, and demolish
The walls of our temporal body, the walls of our souls that
   are blinded,
So that at last we may see that which here remains hidden.
Freedom, how long we have sought thee in discipline,
   action and suffering;
Dying, we now may behold thee revealed in the Lord.

DIETRICH BONHOEFFER

$\mathscr{B}$eing with someone during their last breath is a miracle I can't explain. You know what it's like to experience a baby's first breath—it's an experience so amazing you think, "God must exist." It's just as powerful when you witness a person's last breath. You feel so close to God because the person right then is passing into his presence.

LINDA THOMPSON BOMAR

I was there at my mother's last breath. It was so quiet. I remember immediately looking up and feeling a huge weight lifted off my shoulders. She had been suffering, but all of a sudden, she was at peace. Though I had tears in my eyes, I was smiling.

<small>CHRIS MCCANN</small>

*S*uddenly her fingers tightened on mine. She said in a clear weak voice: "Oh, dearling, look…." She didn't go on, if there was more. I knew that if I said, "What is it?" she would make an effort and go on; but I did not do so. I don't know why I didn't. She might have been saying, "look," as one who suddenly understands something, or as one who beholds— what?… And I shall not know this side of eternity, for they were her last words: "Oh, dearling, look!"

<small>SHELDON VANAUKEN</small>

*T*hen I saw a new heaven and a new earth; for the first heaven and the first earth passed away…. I saw the Holy City, the new Jerusalem, coming down out of heaven from God, prepared as a bride beautifully dressed for her husband. And I heard a loud voice from the throne saying, "Now the dwelling of God is with men, and he will live with them. They will be his people, and God himself will be with them and be their God. He will wipe every tear from their eyes. There will be no more death or mourning or crying or pain, for the old order of things has passed away."

<small>REVELATION 21:1-4, *NIV*</small>

There are more things in heaven and earth, Horatio, than are dreamt of in your philosophy.

WILLIAM SHAKESPEARE, *Hamlet*

Do not let your hearts be troubled. Trust in God; trust also in me. In my Father's house are many rooms; if it were not so, I would have told you. I am going to prepare a place for you.

JOHN 14:1-2, *NIV*

Why do we all love stories that end "happily ever after?" Because the truth is that we are meant to have "happily ever after." But it doesn't apply to our time on earth. It applies to our time to come in heaven.

PASTOR DEAN HONNETTE

For our homeland is in heaven, and from heaven comes the Savior we are waiting for, the Lord Jesus Christ, who, by the power that enables him to bring everything under his control, will transform our lowly bodies so that they will be like his glorious body.

PHILIPPIANS 3:20-21

*B*eing "glorified"—I know the meaning of that now. It's the time, after my death here, when I'll be dancing on my feet.

JONI EARECKSON TADA, paralyzed from the neck down in a diving accident

God doesn't give us pain for no reason; it has a purpose. Offer your pain back to God and watch Him turn it into a glorious reward. Be obedient to His leading, for surely He is leading you to find healing in His everlasting arms. He is Jehovah Rapha—the God who heals. If you allow Him, He will transform your pain into an 'eternal weight of glory'.

LYNN SMITH DERBYSHIRE

I shall hear in Heaven

LUDWIG VAN BEETHOVEN, last words

The body of
Benjamin Franklin, Printer,
Like the cover of an old book,
Its contents torn out,
And script of its lettering and gilding,
Lies here, food for worms,
But the work shall not be lost,
For it will, as he believ'd,
Appear once more
In a new and more elegant edition,
Corrected and improved
By the Author

BENJAMIN FRANKLIN, epitaph he wrote for his gravestone

I consider that our present sufferings are not worth comparing with the glory that will be revealed in us.

ROMANS 8:18, *NIV*

*O*h Lord. Almighty God. Hit ain't for us ignorant mortals to say what's right and what's wrong. Was any one of us to be a-doin' of it, we'd not of brung this pore boy into the world a cripple, and his mind teched. We'd of brung him in straight and tall like his brothers, fitten to live and work and do. But in a way o' speakin', Lord, you done made it up to him. You give him a way with the wild creeturs. You give him a sort o' wisdom, made him knowin' and gentle. The birds come to him, and the varmints moved free about him, and like as not he could o' takened a she wild-cat right in his pore twisted hands.

"Now you've done seed fit to take him where bein' crookedy in mind or limb don't matter. But Lord, hit pleasures us to think now you've done straightened out them legs and that pore bent back and them hands. Hit pleasure us to think on him, movin' around as easy as any one. And Lord, give him a few red-birds and mebbe a squirrel and a 'coon and a 'possum to keep him comp'ny, like he had here. All of us is somehow lonesome, and we know he'll not be lonesome, do he have them leetle wild things around him, if it ain't askin' too much to put a few varmints in heaven. Thy will be done. Amen."

MARJORIE KINNAN RAWLINGS, *The Yearling*

*G*od forbid that I should go to any heaven in which there are no horses.

ROBERT BONTINE CUNNINGHAME-GRAHAM, from a letter to Theodore Roosevelt

I hope with all my heart there will be painting in heaven.

CAROT, 19th century painter, last words

*W*hen his earthly work is done,
Look kindly on the work nut.
And in heaven's pasture, Lord,
Leave a little grass to cut.

PATRICIA S. RUTTER

*H*ere lie I, Martin Elginbrodde:
Have mercy on my soul, Lord God,
As I would do, were I Lord God
and You were Martin Elginbrodde.

EPITAPH in Elgin Cathedral

*T*he human body is a psychosomatic unity (*psyche*-soul;
soma-body), and as such is subject to death. The entire
human being dies, and the entire human being is given a
new bodily existence by God in the resurrection of the dead.
The resurrection of the dead is God's gift; it is in no way an
inherent capacity of the human being.

THE REV. FLEMING RUTLEDGE

*B*e comforted; it is not from yourself that you must expect
it, but on the contrary, you must expect it by expecting nothing
from yourself.

BLAISE PASCAL

Amazing Grace

Amazing grace! how sweet the sound
That saved a wretch like me!
I once was lost, but now am found,
Was blind, but now I see.

'Twas grace that taught my heart to fear,
And grace my fears relieved;
How precious did that grace appear
The hour I first believed!

Through many dangers toils and snares
I have already come;
It's grace that brought me safe thus far
And grace will lead me home.

When we've been there ten thousand years,
Bright shining as the sun,
We've no less days to sing God's praise
Than when we first begun.

JOHN NEWTON

God's purpose is not death, but resurrection.

THE REV. ROSS WRIGHT

Every parting gives a foretaste of death; every coming
together again a foretaste of the resurrection.

ARTHUR SCHOPENHAUER

$\mathcal{D}$uring Pops last few weeks of life, we talked about heaven being a perfect place. We also talked about the fallibility of man. Then I said, "Pops, because we're imperfect, if we were to go to heaven, it wouldn't be a perfect place anymore, would it?" Pops laughed a "no" that revealed an all-too-familiar recognition of his shortcomings. His eyes and the squeeze of his hand told me he was eager for the answer to this dilemma. I paraphrased John 3:16 and explained that God sent Jesus to pay the penalty for all our sins. If we ask for His forgiveness and open our hearts to him, he will make us clean and perfect inside. With a humble heart, my 94-year-old grandfather bowed his head and did just that.

SCOTT JOHNSTON

$\mathcal{F}$or God so loved the world that he gave his one and only Son, that whoever believes in him shall not perish but have eternal life. For God did not send his Son into the world to condemn the world, but to save the world through him.

JOHN 3:16-17, *NIV*

$\mathcal{G}$ive joy or grief give ease or pain
Take life and friends away
But let me find them all again
In the eternal day

Gravestone in memory of 3 children of Jones & Sarah Dennis, 1781, 1792, 1802

You cannot tell the unhappy person that he or she has nothing to worry about because at the end of life he will become absorbed in some kind of collective unconscious.... What sort of a God would it be who would absorb us into Himself and snuff out our own individuality in the process?... Life either has meaning for me, for my own personal speck of cosmic dust existence, or it has no meaning at all.

ANDREW GREELEY, *Death and Beyond*

This is really not so difficult to understand. Scientists tell us that the body is constantly wearing away and reproducing itself.... The actual atoms that make up our body now are different from those in our body four or five years ago. And the substance of the soft parts is completely exchanged every few months. Yet we know that our body is the identical one we had last year.

Perhaps the same thing will be true of our resurrected bodies. We do not know the chemical composition of that body, but.... it will be just as much our body as our body today is the one we had a year ago. It will be our body because it will be perfectly suited to us and to our spirit.

KENNETH S. KANTZER

Heaven and Earth are threads of one loom.

ANONYMOUS BROTHER of the Shaker faith

A rose will still
be a rose in heaven,
it will just smell ten
times sweeter.

PEGGY WOODSON

*H*ope looks beyond the bonds of time,
When what we now deplore,
Shall rise in full immortal prime,
And bloom to fade no more.

Gravestone in memory of Mary Owens Dodd, 1825

$\mathcal{O}$ur Lord has written the promise of resurrection,
not in books alone, but in every leaf of springtime.

MARTIN LUTHER

$\mathcal{O}$N MY CHILD'S DEATH

Clocks strike in the distance,
Already the night grows late,
How dimly the lamp glistens;
Your bed is all made.

It is the wind goes, only,
Grieving around the house;
Where, inside, we sit lonely
Often listening out.

It is as if, how lightly,
You must be going to knock,
Had missed your way and might be
Tired, now, coming back.

We are poor, poor stupid folk!
It's we, still lost in dread,
Who wander in the dark—
You've long since found your bed.

JOSEPH VON EICHENDORF

$\mathcal{S}$he is with me, as real as the winter snow that blends
the tears upon my face. And it is only when I try to touch her,
to make her linger yet awhile, that she dies all over again.

SAMANTHA MOONEY, *A Snowflake In My Hand*

Remember me when I am gone away,
Gone far away into the silent land;
When you can no more hold me by the hand,
Nor I half turn to go, yet turning stay.

Yet if you should forget me for a while
And afterwards remember, do not grieve:
For if the darkness and corruption leave
A vestige of the thoughts that once I had,
Better by far you should forget and smile
Than that you should remember and be sad.

CHRISTINA ROSSETTI

The goal is to strike that delicate balance between the past
that should be remembered and a future that must be created.

EARL A. GROLLMAN, *Talking About Death*

Depression is boring I think, and I would do better
to make some soup and light up the cave.

ANNE SEXTON

Peace; come away: the song of woe
Is after all an earthly song.
Peace; come away: we do him wrong
To sing so wildly: let us go.

ALFRED, LORD TENNYSON

Do you know what the last words she spoke to me were?
She opened her great big, wondrous Italian eyes, and saw me
with tears running down my cheeks and she said—imagine
this—"Felice, what are you holding on to?"

LEO F. BUSCAGLIA, *Living, Loving and Learning*

Mama has died. I am left with all the good she did for me
and all the bad I did to her.

ALEXANDER SOLZHENITYSN

Missing him now, I am haunted by my own shortcomings,
how often I failed him. I think every parent must have a sense
of failure, even of sin, merely in remaining alive after the death
of a child. One feels that it is not right to live when one's child
has died, that one should somehow have found the way to give
one's life to save his life. Failing there, one's failures during his
too brief life seem all the harder to bear and forgive....

I wish we had loved Johnny more when he was alive.
Of course we loved Johnny very much. Johnny knew that.
Everybody knew it. Loving Johnny more. What does it mean?
What can it mean, now?

FRANCES GUNTHER, excerpt from John Gunther's memoir of their son

If only," he said—two words with which all who have lost a loved one must come to terms.

JANE BURGESS KOHN, *The Widower*

I was not at her bedside
that final day, I did not grant her ancient,
huge-knuckled hand
its last wish, I did not let it
gradually become empty of the son's hand—and so
hand her, with more steadiness, into the future.

I know now there are regrets
we can never be rid of;
permanent remorse. Knowing this, I know also
I am to draw from that surplus stored up
of tenderness which was hers by right,
and which no one ever gave her,
and give it away, freely.

GALWAY KINNELL, *Mortal Acts, Mortal Words*

Is there any stab as deep as wondering where and how
you failed those you loved?

FLORIDA SCOTT-MAXWELL

*I*n the early 1970s I counseled many young men returning to college after combat in Vietnam. I was astonished at how many of these men felt guilty for coming home alive. As one highly decorated soldier put it, "I knew and loved better men than me who died there."

In almost every situation it is outside the realm of anybody's power to determine which persons live or die. You need not impose on yourself a penalty for your own life and health and good fortune simply because others suffer terribly. We can live useful lives in appreciation of our own health and continuing existence. No more than that is required of us.

ANN KAISER STERNS, *Living Through Personal Crisis*

*T*he heart's affections are divided like the branches of the cedar tree; if the tree loses one strong branch, it will suffer but it does not die. It will pour all its vitality into the next branch so that it will grow and fill the empty space." This is what your mother told me when her father died, and you should say the same thing when death takes my body to its resting place and my soul to God's care.

KAHLIL GIBRAN, *The Broken Wings*

I lost a dear friend to cancer. One of the last things he said to me was "Tommy, do what's right." Now he knew that doing right doesn't earn God's love which is always there for us. But it does make a better life for me and my family. When I'm faced with a difficult choice, I often "hear" his voice saying, "Tommy, do what's right."

TOM PATITUCCI

I have often heard such criticisms leveled at widows and widowers who; instead of sinking into gloom, remain active and serene.

I think there is a certain amount of psychological over-compensation in my present activity, and in my writing so many books. All my work, in any case, could be interpreted as a "work of mourning." But I find in it a sort of fellowship with Nelly: we did everything together, and in a way we still do. I have a strong sense of her invisible spirit... There are widowers who, as it were, suspend their lives, as if life had stopped at the moment of their bereavement. Their present thoughts have turned toward the past, whereas I live in the present and look to the future.

For some, therefore, it is, if anything, a retrograde and paralyzing presence, whereas my wife's presence is living and stimulating.

PAUL TOURNIER, *Creative Suffering*

Am I healing? I'm able to gaze at her photograph without that tourniquet tightening around my throat.... I'm beginning to see her in *her* life, and not only myself bereft of her life....

Piece by piece, I reenter the world. A new phase. A new body, a new voice. Birds console me by flying, trees by growing, dogs by the warm patch they leave behind on the sofa. Unknown people merely by performing their motions. It's like a slow recovery from a sickness, this recovery of one's self.... My mother was at peace. She was ready. A free woman. "Let me go," she said. Okay, Mama. I'm letting you go.

TOBY TALBOT, *A Book About My Mother*

GOODNIGHT, WILLIE LEE. I'LL SEE YOU IN THE MORNING

Looking down into my father's
dead face
for the last time
my mother said without
tears, without smiles
without regrets
but with *civility*
"Goodnight, Willie Lee, I'll see you
in the morning."
And it was then I knew that the healing
of all our wounds
is forgiveness
that permits a promise
of our return
at the end.

ALICE WALKER

She said not "good-bye" but "forgive me".... The two words (in Russian) are practically interchangeable! It is the profoundest, the last good-bye.

ANNE MORROW LINDBERGH, *War Within And Without*

$\mathcal{A}$ small boy's dog was killed by an automobile. His first reaction was one of shock and dismay, followed by outrage against his parents. He felt they were guilty because they had not taken proper care of the pet. (The boy behaved like an adult who rages against God for neglecting His charges.) Yet anger against the parents was a substitute for his own guilt, for the youngster had on occasion wished to be rid of "that awful pest." The child insisted that one of his favorite toys be buried with the dog. The toy served as a kind of peace offering to the offended pet. Now the lad was freed of anxiety and could continue to function effectively in his everyday activities. Ritual combined the dynamics of guilt, assuagement, and reparation—similar to the mourning behavior of adults.

EARL A. GROLLMAN, *Talking About Death*

$\mathcal{M}$y heart was heavy, for its trust had been
Abused, its Kindness answered with foul wrong:
So, turning gloomily from my fellow-men,
One summer Sabbath-day, I strolled among
The green mounds of the village burial place;
Where, pondering how all human love and hate
Find one sad level, and how, soon or late,
Wronged and wrongdoer, each with meekened face
And cold hands folded over a still heart,
Pass the green threshold of our common grave,
Wither all footsteps tend, whence none depart,
Awed for myself and pitying my race,
Our common sorrow, like a mighty wave,
Swept all my pride away, and, trembling, I forgave.

JOHN GREENLEAF WHITTIER

Forgiveness is the fragrance that the violet sheds
on the heal that has crushed it.

MARK TWAIN

Let Jew and Gentile, meeting
From many a distant shore,
Around one altar kneeling,
One common Lord adore.
Let all that now divides us
Remove and pass away,
Like shadows of the morning
Before the blaze of day

HENRY SMART

And throughout all eternity
I forgive you, you forgive me.

WILLIAM BLAKE

One Sunday when I was struggling with this, the Scripture
reading came from the sixth chapter of Luke: "Forgive, and ye
shall be forgiven." Now, try as I might, I cannot find a loophole
in that. It does not say, "Forgive everyone, unless they've said
something rude about your child." And it doesn't even say,
"Just *try*." It says, If you want to be forgiven, if you want to
experience that kind of love, you have to forgive everyone in
your life—everyone, even the very worst boyfriend you ever
had—even, for God's sake, yourself.

ANNE LAMOTT, *Traveling Mercies*

*W*hen Bill was admitted I sensed his anger. He was hostile and abrupt. And very restless. When he finally fell asleep he would moan as if something terribly wrong had happened.

I asked him if everything was O.K. He didn't answer. So I asked again. No response. It was then that I knew he had some unfinished business that needed to be completed if he was to die a good death.

His physical signs were rapidly deteriorating. But he wouldn't die. He wouldn't let go. It was as if there was something deep within him that would not permit death.

I talked to his son: "Something very deep is bothering your dad. I don't know what it is. But unless it is resolved your father will never die in peace."

The son's eyes filled with tears. The family secret was about to be told.

"I am not the only child. I have a sister who lives in Baltimore, Maryland. My dad disowned her nine years ago because she married someone of another race. From his point of view, she committed the unpardonable sin. He said he would never forgive her."

When I heard that confession I knew what his unfinished business was all about. I told the son to call his sister and tell her to get to Minneapolis as fast as possible.

Five hours later she arrived. I went with them to their father's room. For the first time in nine years he saw his daughter. He said nothing but just stared at her. Then he opened his arms to his daughter and with all the strength that was left in that frail body hugged her. She brushed away his tears and sat on the bed. They said nothing for the longest time.

Finally he looked into her eyes and said two words that freed him forever: "I'm sorry."

There were many tears. They held one another and talked about old times. The dad learned that he was a grandfather and there was much laughter.

I checked his vital signs later that evening and they seemed stronger. But then an amazing thing happened.

Around 10:30 P.M. the father said that he was very tired. But he didn't want the children to leave the room. I sensed what was about to happen and told the son and daughter to stay.

Each child held his hand. And then he died. But his expression was serene. The bitterness was gone. Grievances had been resolved. All unfinished business put to rest.

ROBERT L. VENINGA, *A Gift of Hope*

*I*t is important that when we come to die we have nothing to do but to die.

CHARLES HODGE

*W*hy, she asked herself, why keep a wound open when forgiveness can close it?

ALEXANDER MCCALL SMITH, *The Full Cupboard of Life*

*F*orgiveness is trusting God to help you heal.

PASTOR DEAN HONNETTE

There is a kind of release
And a kind of torment in every goodbye
for every man.

C. DAY LEWIS

You have grown wings of pain
and flap around the bed like a wounded gull
calling for water, calling for tea, for grapes
whose skins you cannot penetrate.
Remember when you taught me
how to swim? Let go, you said,
the lake will hold you up.
I long to say, Father let go
and death will hold you up…

LINDA PASTAN

*O*ne does not discover new lands
without consenting to lose sight of the shore…

ANDRÉ GIDE

*S*unset and evening star,
  And one clear call for me!
And may there be no moaning of the bar,
  When I put out to sea,

But such a tide as moving seems asleep,
  Too full for sound and foam,
When that which drew from out the boundless deep
  Turns again home.

Twilight and evening bell,
  And after that the dark!
And may there be no sadness of farewell,
  When I embark;

For tho' from out our bourne of Time and Place
  The flood may bear me far,
I hope to see my Pilot face to face
  When I have crost the bar.

ALFRED, LORD TENNYSON

*A*dieu, mes amis. Je vais la gloire.
(Farewell, my friends! I go to glory!)

ISADORA DUNCAN, Dancer, last words

*O*nce a year in church, we sing the spiritual, "We Shall Overcome" in remembrance of Dr. Martin Luther King, Jr. Each year I tell myself I will not cry when we sing this simple song. Each year I cry. This song leads me to think about my life and events over the past year. My blood family, church family, friends, neighbors, colleagues have all experienced joys and struggles through the year. There have been illnesses, surgeries, new babies, birthdays, deaths, job losses, new jobs, leavings, new friendships, spiritual highs and dark nights of the soul. The repetitive nature of this song drills to my heart. The plight of the slaves in past years comes to mind. Their hope was so powerful that in the midst of hopelessness, they believed that they would overcome. Their faith was so strong that they knew their God would not forsake them and would take them into His Kingdom some day. Their love was so strong that they knew others would link arms with them in their walk to freedom. It is uncanny to me that one simple song can carry me so far into hopelessness, pain and suffering, and at the same time lift me up with hope, love, peace and ultimate joy. Finally, I remember the words of Jesus to his disciples in John 16:33. "These things I have spoken to you that in me you might have peace. In the world you shall have tribulation, but take courage; I have overcome the world." So although I cry every year we sing this song in church, I leave the service with a greater sense of community, inner strength, and knowledge that God is with each of us individually and collectively in our joys and tribulations. I am overcome.

JILL PERRY RABIDEAU

We shall overcome
We shall overcome
We shall overcome one day
Oh, deep in my heart
I do believe
That we shall overcome one day

AFRO-AMERICAN SPIRITUAL

Let goods and kindred go,
This mortal life also;
The body they may kill:
God's truth abideth still;
His kingdom is forever.

MARTIN LUTHER, from the hymn, "A Mighty Fortress"

Night is drawing nigh—"
For all that has been—Thanks!
To all that shall be—Yes!

DAG HAMMARSKJÖLD, *Markings*

ACKNOWLEDGEMENTS

The editors are enormously grateful to all contributors to this book, many of whom are not credited below, but are friends and inspirations just as worthy.

Every effort has been made to obtain permissions for previously printed material. If anything in the credits appears to be amiss, please notify us at info@cupolapress.com so that proper credit can be given in subsequent printings.

Excerpts from A CIRCLE OF QUIET by Madeleine L'Engle. Copyright © 1972 by Madeleine L'Engle Franklin. Reprinted by permission of Farrar, Straus and Giroux, LLC.

Excerpt from A DEATH IN THE FAMILY by James Agee. Copyright © 1957 by The James Agee Trust, renewed © 1985 by Mia Agee. Used by permission of Grosset & Dunlap, Inc., a division of Penguin Group (USA) Inc.

Excerpts from A GIFT OF HOPE: HOW WE SURVIVE OUR TRAGEDIES by Robert Veninga. Copyright © 1985 by Robert L. Veninga, Little, Brown and Company.

Excerpts from A NOT ENTIRELY BENIGH PROCEDURE by Perri Klass. Copyright © 1987 by Perri Klass. Used by permission of G.P. Putnam's Sons, a division of Penguin Group (USA) Inc.

Excerpts from A SEVERE MERCY by Sheldon Vanauken. Copyright © 1977, 1980 by Sheldon Vanauken. Reprinted by permission of HarperCollins Publishers.

Excerpt from THE ADVENTURE OF LIVING by Paul Tournier. Copyright © 1965 by Paul Tournier. Reprinted by permission of HarperCollins Publishers.

Excerpt from AGING by Henri J.M. Nouwen and Walter J. Gaffney. Copyright © 1974 by Henri J.M. Nouwen and Walter J. Gaffney. Photos © 1974 by Ron P. Van den Bosch. Used by permission of Doubleday, a division of Random House, Inc.

Excerpt from ALL RIVERS RUN TO THE SEA by Elie Wiesel. Copyright © 1995 by Alfred A. Knopf, Inc. Used by permission of Alfred A. Knopf, a division of Random House, Inc.

Excerpt from "ASH WEDNESDAY" in COLLECTED POEMS 1909-1962 by T. S. Eliot. Copyright 1930 by Harcourt, Inc., and renewed 1958 by T. S. Eliot. Reprinted by permission of the publisher.

Excerpt by REINE DUELL BETHANY. Copyright 1986 *Christian Century*. Reprinted by permission from the April 4, 1986, issue of the *Christian Century*. Subscriptions: $49/yr. from P.O. Box 378, Mt. Morris, IL 61054. 1-800-208-4097.

Excerpt by DIETRICH BONHOEFFER reprinted with the permission of Scribner, an imprint of Simon & Schuster Adult Publishing Group, from LETTERS AND PAPERS FROM PRISON, REVISED, ENLARGED ED. by Dietrich Bonhoeffer (Translated from the German by R.H. Fuller, Frank Clark, et al). Copyright © 1953, 1967, 1971 by SCM Press Ltd. All rights reserved.

Poem by NEAL BOWERS. First published in the *Sewanee Review,* vol. 93, no. 1, winter 1985. Copyright 1985 by Neal Bowers. Reprinted with the permission of the editor and the author.

ABOUT THE EDITORS

Gail Perry Johnston is the owner of P. Johnston Design & Advertising in the San Francisco Bay Area. She recently formed Cupola Press for the purpose of using her design skills to bring meaningful literary works to light. *A Rumor of Angels* was inspired by her love of a well-turned phrase, her faith in a personal God who offers life after death, and her need to process her own losses. Her second collection, *The Wish & The Wonder: Words of Wisdom for Expectant Parents,* offers insight, wit and encouragement for those expecting a baby. Gail and her husband, Scott Johnston, are blessed to be the parents of Luke and Shelby.

Jill Perry Rabideau, MHA, M.S., OTR/L is a general partner at Children's Therapy Associates in Natick, MA. With 25 years of experience working with children who have special needs, Jill has consistently involved herself in the hardship of her students and their families. She believes that to share pain and to encourage hope is to love. Jill and her husband, Gary Rabideau, are blessed to be the parents of Bryce and Ali.

Cupola
PRESS™

We are a new publisher and welcome feedback. Please visit
www.cupolapress.com and send us your comments about
A Rumor of Angels. Inspirational gifts developed from quotes
and images in this book can also be found on our site.